Stoicism

What Can Stoicism Teach You About the Art of Living and How to Achieve Success in Modern Life? Discover a Powerful Ancient Tool to Grow a Stronger Mind, Boost your Confidence and Resilience

Dr. Kevin Carol Miyake

Table of Contents

Introduction: Stoicism and Its Philosophers

Sometimes life is very dull because you work hard on an issue, but you are unpleasantly reimbursed. Moreover, life seems to favor those who do not deserve the credit and disfavors those who are equally deserving of the opportunity. What comes out of those misfortunes is pain and desperation. However, Zeno of Citium developed an ideology of stoicism which was designed to deal with those life misgivings. This philosophy stated that the human path is engrossed with pain, where one has to accept that situation as it presents itself. In that case, one should embrace endurance and not be controlled with the pleasures and sufferings of this world. These scholars identified that eudaimonia was the critical parameter in the persons living.

To gain such happiness, you were obliged to behave virtually. That meant one ought to act according to the right morals. Therefore, the stoics indicated that virtue attitude is internal, but external things such as riches and materialistic desires were not of significant concern. Other scholars like Epictetus, Seneca and Marcus Aurelius acknowledged that nature controlled like every social situation. Therefore, judgment was supposed to be vindicated upon the behavior of a person rather than their words.

They concluded that nature controlled everything that happened in this world.

Therefore, the stoic ideology is very paramount even today because various principles govern it. This principle includes nature, the law of reason, virtue, wisdom, and duty, which should be sought and not the sake of pleasure.

Chapter 1: Philosophy: A Powerful Tool to Succeed In the Modern World and Help You Achieve Eudaimonia

Perhaps the best thing in this life is to feel happy. When you are so glad it means you are contented with what you have. Other people may say that you are stress-free. However, the earlier philosophers in the likes of Socrates, Plato, Aristotle, and many others considered the act of happiness is achieved by doing virtuous behaviors. A virtue belief is a morally upright quality needed in society. These characteristics include piety, selflessness, patience, kindness, humility, and many other attributes. Therefore, this attitude of happiness is referred to as eudemonia.

You may have met a beggar who is very enthusiastic or happy. Such a person may not have that materialistic wealth or luxury but is virtuous. That illustration may be hard to understand because many people view the wealthy class to be happy enjoys life. However, that is not the case because you may be a distressful tycoon. Therefore, it is all about feeling comfortable and knowing your capabilities. In the case of that humble beggar, he or she is showing signs of excellence, happiness, and confident of greatness in the future. Therefore, that shows that living a happy life is brought by doing right no matter the situation you have

How Does Philosophy Relate to Eudaimonia?

Many are the times where humans try to gain knowledge of the fundamental nature of a substance. Due to philosophy, science and arot were developed. That is because early humans tried to describe why certain situations existed the way they are. Therefore, philosophy is the study of the nature of knowledge, reality, or existence. In that case, the philosophers tried to learn the right virtues to apply in gaining the wellbeing of an individual. It is common for all humans to want to live in peaceful and actualize their dreams. However, these dreams and happiness may be in contrast with that of others. That is because what you regard virtuous may be a vice in some sense. Therefore, scholars like Aristotle thought that if virtue is limited or in excess will turn to be a vice. Consequently, the right person must be moderate in practicing good things.

Some Examples of These Philosophical Virtues That Are Moderated

You ought to consider the courage attitude at first. When you are brave, it means you are bold, and you take risks. Therefore, nothing can scare you, which is of good quality. Remember that courageous people score highly, especially in field likes military, hunting, or entrepreneurs who are risk-takers. However, this virtue has its overindulgence as recklessness. Imagine if once lions attacked you, where someone tries to confront those animals unshielded. Then that person is reckless because probably he will be eaten. Other people possess cowardice behavior where they are scared of an incoming danger instead of trying to combat that situation.

The feeling of being comfortable or satisfied is right; however, it may turn up to vice if you are over happy. When in this situation, you can express arrogance and pride. That is where you will view yourself as superior to others. The limited option of this attitude is low self-esteem. When you have low self-worth, you will despise yourself and discredit your prowess.

The virtue of being empathetic is a sign of fruitful living. However, you stand a loss if you are over caring for others and forget your pains. That is, even if your life is going well, you feel stigmatized by the worries of others. The limitless of being empathetic will lead to being wicked and uncaring of the values of others.

Being intelligent makes one happy as you acquire that critical and creative thinking. Nonetheless, remember that there are some cases of being too bright. That is where you will have a manipulative and egocentric spirit of conning and blackmailing others. That does not mean you should be gullible and look like a fool. It is because you will be easily cheated and lured to a trap. Therefore, having a moderate attitude in everything is enough.

Honesty is credited with being transparent upon what you say or do. However, this character stands between being tactless and being a liar. Think of a court scenario, where you are needed to lie in some situations so that your charges will be deducted. If you are too truthful in that case, it means you have no tactics of escaping the punishment.

When you are patient, it means you are optimistic that remarkable things will favor you. That does not warrant you to be impatient and try to do things in a rush. Remember that doing things quick creates chances for an error. At other times if you are too tolerable, you will lose a valuable opportunity that is urgent.

Tips of How to Achieve Eudaimonia through Philosophy

You must know your goals and targets. Remember that the goals are the long-term ambitions and the targets are the daily objectives. In this case, virtues are routine, which should match the goals you want to harness. You may be that humanitarian person who likes helping the needy. You will consequently identify your intentions of wanting to improve the lives of many people. The attributes may also be regarded as your visions of what you want to do. Therefore, if you feel your life is taking to that course that is when you feel overjoyed.

One also has to focus on individual talents and capabilities. Most are the times your prowess is tested when you meet yourself in a dilemma situation. You may be that professional doctor called up to be that humanitarian. You have to choose to serve others voluntarily or receive that Ransom salary. However, go for the choice that is your passion even if it is not paying well. That is why you will find most people leaving lucrative offers to go for a poor paying job. If you ask them why they did so, they tell you that they were following their heart desires which sometimes is the right thing to do. In this part, you have to focus on individual expertise and areas that give you room for self-development.

You still have to develop your talents. That is after knowing the capabilities and skills needed in that area. The art of practicing something frequently will enlighten you on how best to perform that action. You also have to dig of information concerning the are to ensure the services you render are quality. While doing so, you may reduce any cases of error and any complication of your carrier. The state of Eudaimonia will be improved if you gain expertise in your field of specialization. You will realize that you are increasing steps to reaching your self-actualization platform. At this stage, you have improved your self-esteem and confidence

Actively getting engaged in those services improves your eudaimonia. Take an example of a humanitarian who helps the needy people. Your wishes are creating a positive impact on the lives of those individuals. Actively engaging the needy makes you feel joyous and responsible for their wants. You will realize that been active in those areas will create a hobby in what you want. You know how one feels doing the things you desire; you will feel enthusiastic. Other people have discovered eve their talents by actively engaging in their hobbies. Therefore, it is upon you to know which activity entices you mostly.

Always express yourself. That is not just the word of your mouth but your action. You will be judged by the many lives you have touched in that charitable event or the impact you made when doing the right thing. The moral impact you made on your business still will speak for you. Remember that Eudaimonia is about a feeling of happiness; therefore, at this point, you will obtain maximum pleasure in yourself.

What are some of the signs of Eudaimonia people?

What is mostly associated with eudemonic is happiness. These people have no sense of distress. Their lives seem like a happy riding as they are enthusiastic all the time. Hey, that does not mean they do not face problems, but, they persevere to any stalemates. Being happy also means they are positive about their life story.

They are individuals who listen to other ideas. That means they take credit upon the information of another. Consequently, they are not boastful of their success but like to hear how others say about them. Moreover, being a state of wellbeing means that you are at peace with others. You can achieve this by listening to their ideas. If those people realize you have no interest in listening to them they will term you as being arrogant, which is a vice. You will certainly gain knowledge from their feedback which they give to you.

Volunteering for specific tasks means that you are happy at what you are doing. Volunteering means that you are sacrificing the chance to get capital for charitable deeds. These people know that if they help the needy people, which is the right thing. They thereof support people wholeheartedly without asking for any returns. Volunteering for services will also include one giving money to those in need.

Another sign with them is that they are always authentic. These people are real and assertive about what they believe. They show faith in their actions which they are satisfied that those actions bring good results. Sometimes they are criticized for their deeds; however, they do not falter if they believe that the acts are productive. By guarding their virtues firmly even when rejected shows how authentic they are.

Eudaimonia people show excellence in what they do. That is a sign that they are satisfied with the career or profession they take. Generally, if you love something, you will work hard to produce good results. Before you realize it, you will make a habit of repeating the excellent performance of those activities. In that regard, much success is achieved.

Such individuals are knowledgeable. That is where they like seeking for information to improve their expertise level. They will feel satisfied when they can answer any question directed to them. They do also take positively of any challenge poised to them. Sometimes being interactive with people will give your ideas, where these fellows prefer.

Moderation is a consistent characteristic associated with eudaimonia feeling. Scholars say that ' too much of something is poisonous.' Yes, this sounds right because these fellows will always want to limit themselves upon anything. If they are charitable, it does not mean they will give out everything and forget themselves. Moreover, doing less of something can also be harmful. Therefore, moderation accords them of the quality of being sustainable and sufficient.

They have that self-discipline and acceptance. That is where these people are responsible for their acts that should not hurt anybody else. They realize their potential and accept their success. Even if they feel they always take corrections

Chapter 2: The Spiritual Side of Stoicism

From a religious point of view, stoicism is desire to advocate for personal reverence instead of public worship. Worship and prayer were undoubtedly used in the peace of stoicism and their primary goal was to incline the actions and thoughts of each specialist into an agreement with universal logos (reason) that permeates the cosmos. Similarly, Pierre Hadot a philosopher from France argues that, above everything else, a stoic could be primarily identified by the type of life they choose to live, in which case every action, thought, desire would be controlled entirely by the law of universal reason.

The goal of inclining human nature to cosmos as the gateway to well-being and virtue is extremely clear from the texts that talk about stoicism to the extent that nobody had ever thought of denying until the agonists and atheists of the modern world launched the campaign to conform stoic practices to their point of view. In as much as a series of profound differences separate stoic practices from traditional monotheistic religions, the theological language of Epictetus asserts that individual experience and belief that is deeply rooted and bona fide as that of any Muslim, Jew or Christian.

Similarly, Christoph Jedan, a German professor of ethics argues that the religious gist of practicing Stoicism in philosophy provides the gateway for an extensive understanding the ethics of Stoicism not only from a structural viewpoint but also across time, by aiding us to grasp a series of unreasonable and ostensibly statements of Stoicism.

From the traditional point of view, stoicism cannot be classified as a religion; nonetheless, it is a thoroughly spiritual way of life drafted to remodel the practitioner. Stoicism remodels practitioners by changing their idea of what is bad and what is good by tutoring them to live a life characterized by moral excellence in accordance with the cosmic nature. Simply put, a stoic is somebody who is one strives to abide by the will of God.

The cosmic providence and spirituality of Stoicism might be regarded as false belief and practice by modern-day academics and it might be a turn off to agonists and atheists who angrily seek agonists and atheists who strive to individually identity themselves as stoics of the modern era of secularization. However, the cosmos is depicted as omnipresent in the texts of Stoicism, and that it forms a crucial aspect of the practice and theory of stoicism. To Seneca, the "God within" was very important; the talk about God by Epictetus was a way of expressing his reverence towards as well as the relationship with the divine state of nature; that is why in the discretion of his journal Marcus was relentless in making it clear that it is pointless living in a world that lacks gods or lacks Providence.

Seneca did not see the reason for being alive or the worth of life if God and his capability to envisage divine were not in existence. Certainly, Epictetus displays his personal piety when he suggests the need for us praise God. He says that if he was a swan, he would perform the work of a swan and that if he were a nightingale, he would do what a nightingale does. However, considering the fact that he is a rational being, he must praise God. He goes further to say that this is his task and that he will do everything to accomplish it without fail. From his words, it is evident that Epictetus claims to be an ardent follower of the olden ways of stoat when he insists that every philosopher should acknowledge the existence of God and that it is him who has the ability to providentially administer cosmos. Marcus Aurelius also reflects the same type of reverence as Epictetus based on his deeply-rooted trust in cosmic providence for emotional and ethical support.

Numerous people have been inspired by Marcus Aurelius' meditation and that probably explains why it is still an inspirational and influential part of the Western ethical and spiritual canon beyond the twentieth century into the twenty-first century. One American religious scholar and philosopher is of the suggestion that combining poetic brilliance, mystical visions well as the earthly realism of a leader based on the Marcus Aurelius' meditations, can be a great way to give ourselves inspiration and realistic and forthright hope in our troubled lives. As a result, Marcus goes further to argue that meditation should be accorded a unique part among the works of various legendary spiritual philosophers of the world.

The fact that stoicism is deeply rooted in spirituality is enough evidence to any reader of the existing stoics that is open-minded. No, it is not right to say that stoicism can be categorized as a regularized religion. However, it is crucial to acknowledge that stoicism goes beyond being a life hack, a gateway to tranquility or a stoical kind of mental behavioral therapy. Stoicism is a profoundly philosophical and spiritual way of life. The spiritual part of stoicism continues to be a major influence on numerous moderns simply because it relates to the human nature which instinctively knows that we are all competitors in a course that is mightier than ourselves.

The information contained in the stoic texts gives us the feeling of being gently pulled by cosmic nature which refers to that which we physically belong, but from which we have been detached physically. The planetary nature advocates more for the idea of agreeing with natural events for the sake of our well-being rather than demanding obedience to a set of rules. When we live in agreement with infinite nature, we realize the excellence within our nature as human beings and consequently, we can undergo a state of psychological well-being mindless to any external factors. Despite the misunderstanding of many people of stoicism as a religion, it is and will remain to be a feasible gateway for the majority of moderns. The practices, as well as the spiritual teachings of stoicism, will not direct you to a temple, church, confessional booth, tent revival, alter call or a series of Holy Scriptures. Contrary to that, stoicism will guide you to a sacred place deep inside you. A place where that divine part of you can resuscitate the divinity that is inherent in nature to mold a meaningful and rational life.

That being said, we will now shift our focus into the importance of stoic spiritual exercises that Pierre Hadot referred to as "active" practices of spirituality as well as where these active exercises originated from the three disciplines of Stoicism that Epictetus talked about in his Enchiridion and Discourses. Pierre's "active" exercises of Stoicism include accomplishment of duties, indifference to indifferent things and self-mastery.

Self-Mastery (enkrateia)

Pierre Hadot insists that for somebody to accomplish self-mastery, he/she has to pare down his/her desires and aspirations and strictly restrict them to moral righteousness, which according to him is the only aspect that we have total control over. Similarly, our hostility or unwillingness should be cut down to moral evil. Anything that lies beyond the two spheres named above is not in our jurisdiction whatsoever, therefore, worrying about it is time wasting.

Ancient sources have added further distinctions or gradation of self-mastery. According to Diogenes Laertius, the stoic refers to the apotheosis of self-mastery as well as the autarkeia of being self-sufficient as explained above. Laertius was known for his thriftiness, being contented with poverty, as well as a lonely type of social behavior that was characterized by detachment. Zeno was described as the founder of self-sufficiency by the epigram of Zenodotus. The epigram goes further to say that Zeno gave away his riches and started a school that would, later on, become the beginning of fearless freedom.

Anthony Long says that in as much as Zeno lived in the public eye, the manner in which he depicted his disinterest in the standard signs of success and his extreme contentment with what other people would refer to as ascetism.

According to Long, it is important to note that self-mastery cannot be compared to ataraxic, which is a term that refers to a state of mind that is untroubled, but, however the trio of Hellenistic movements presupposes an ideal of peace for attainment taking into consideration that the basic requirement is having the ability to rationally control somebody's desire.

In as much as the insistence by Zeno made it look like he was relinquishing material possessions, there are numerous things in the world that we could hope that cannot be bought using money. Yes, it is right to say that somebody's well health might to some extent be dependable on his wealth status, but it is common knowledge that even the richest people with superior insurances usually fall sick, and in some instances without or with very minimal recourse.

There are times that you find yourself desiring some calm and quiet environment to read a book. It really comes at no cost but it is something that you desire in which in some cases, you become too much attached. Another example is that you would like your child to act in a certain way, for example, differentially and respectfully. This is also not a material gain but is a need that puts you at the mercy of a six-year-old who might be charming in various ways but in many cases does not put your interest first. Rather than working in reverse doing subtractions in a typical and not –stoic manner of seeing things, the necessary or simply put, the desirable things in life-health, money, status, a peaceful room and an unusually sweet kid-we should do away with all that aside and begin with the least possible and add to that. If we hope to hope to achieve self-mastery, we should only focus on attaining moral virtue. On the other hand, moral evil should be our biggest enemy; all of us should aim at avoiding it.

The accomplishment of duties *{Kathekonta}*

This exercise is different from the other exercises in the sense that it solely relies on other people. It is important to remember that the difference between what is up to us and what is not and to come to the realization that we execute duties for other people, what is in our control is the moral intention we possess as we do it. How our efforts are perceived, whether our bond with the other person grows stronger or whether they have higher expectations from us in future interactions –this is not in our control.

People who are new to stoicism are usually surprised by the social aspect of philosophy because they thought that perhaps it was a way of suppressing emotions and detaching oneself from other people so as to reduce suffering. This is not the best kind of approach because it does not allow us to live according to our nature, the nature of being rational people who have obligations in accordance with the part we usually play parent, friend, citizen or spouse.

To reject or managing to control our own desires can be instrumental when somebody resorts to carrying out duties for other people. If we become too focused on satisfying our own needs, it hinders us from growing ethically. If we spend multiple hours in the office working with the aim of getting a pay rise or promotion, the chances are that in most cases, we will not extend a helping hand to our friends.

Various passages from the Enchiridion come together to give us a sneak peek of various aspects of the stoic commitment to be dutiful helpers to other people. One aspect is that we do not choose our roles; instead, they are assigned to us. We might perceive this as binding, but in a real sense, it basically a reality.

We did not naturally choose to be the children of our parents; we were assigned that role. Another case would be that of citizenship. We do not choose what citizenship to identify with because it is determined by birth. That being said, it is only logical to say that it is pointless to equivocate on our duties. However, it is important to note that the ultimate result is not in our control.

Chapter 3: Stoicism and Psychology

What is the connection, if any, between psychology and stoicism? To better comprehend the relationship between psychology and stoicism, we have to shortly discuss methods of positive psychology as well as its failures and findings. For instance, one major outcome of positive psychology is that it demonstrates a huge difference between what people say makes them happy over a long period of time and their response to moment-to-moment cases. The basic example is the choice to sire children. One section of parents considers siring children a great source of meaning and enrichment in their lives, consequently being instrumental to their sense of succeeding. The other fraction of parents when questioned randomly during the day on what they were up to and how they felt about it, vastly responded that spending time with their children is the most unlikable thing that they go through. They prefer to take up any other activity rather than interacting with their children.

This contradiction, nonetheless would not come as a surprise to a stoic. The stoics were of the impression that the only thing that was really worth going after is moral virtue or righteousness of character. They were aware that from time to time, the situation might result in an unpleasant and painful pursuit. Let us make use of some of Seneca's best examples, Marcus Attilius Regulus the general from Rome to drive the point home. Attilius was taken into captivity by Carthaginians-the lethal enemies of the Roman Empire. The Carthaginians then released him so that he could send a message to Rome; negotiation of a peace treaty on condition that he would go back to Carthage after fulfilling his duty. However, when he arrived in Rome, he pleaded with the Senate not to accept the peace treaty. Thereafter, the protests from citizens of from forcing him to honor his word and go back to Carthage who was disappointed in him and tortured him before executing him by allegedly making him roll down a hill inside a barrel that was hammered with nails from the outside. I am very sure that if a positive psychologist had sought the comments of Attilius on how he felt rolling inside the barrel, and whether the whole painful experience was worth it, he would have given responses that were only ostensibly at odds with one another.

A number of findings of positive psychology directly address the practice of stoicism. For instance, the discovery that vigorous activity in the left part of the prefrontal cortex of the brain has a connection with a stronger capability to revamp positive feelings and conceal the negative feelings. Most importantly, Davidson found out that people can ameliorate activity in that section of the brain, ultimately demonstrating at a level of neurobiology natural mechanism of stoic insistence that we have the ability to train ourselves to avoid consenting to passions that are disruptive.

With reference to stoic practices, researchers in positive psychology discovered that because suffering is part of being a human being, there is a need for people to come up with ways of dealing with it. Fruitful approaches solely depend on breeding strength as well as virtues to reduce the effects of pain. Epictetus would definitely have consented.

Stoicism is not simply a theory; it is a variation of practices that assist people to live better lives. In many instances, the question always is: do Stoic practices really help people? Normally, psychology is usually the only solution to this kind of question. The past fifteen to twenty years have seen the emergence of positive psychology, a branch of psychology that focuses on scientifically educating us off about the good happenings in life and how to improve them for better results. Therefore, in this chapter, we will try to argue with the fact that positive psychology can become wiser or even more complete by absorbing stoic ideas.

Philosophy and positive psychology

In as much as most of the developments between stoicism and positive psychology are exciting, there is the need to ask a couple of crucial questions of philosophy to ask positive psychology:

1. What exactly is the meaning of well-being and what differences being there between well-being and other

connected terms like flourishing, individual well-being, happiness and enjoyment, and pleasure?

2. Positive psychology puts emphasis on doing good as well as feeling good. What is the position or slot for moral virtue in positive psychology?

3. Is it possible that positive behaviors and attitudes really cause harm if they are executed by somebody who is not virtuous?

4. Is wisdom very important like how most contemporary societies thought? Is it not important to simply be optimistic and hopeful but putting into use these qualities in a wise manner?

5. Isi t possible that feasible ideas that were initiated by philosophers such as Epicureans and the stoics be put into the test?

6. Is it possible that strategies of philosophy that have been tested empirically could be used in cultivating virtuous behavior and wisdom as well as enhancing a sense of feeling better with the aim of strengthening positive psychology?

Most of the information in this part of the chapter will focus on most of the questions stated above.

Stoicism as a part of positive psychology

In as much as further research is needed, the series of research that has already been concluded have proven that absorbing stoic practices into the arsenal of techniques that can be used to improve well-being is undoubtedly an excellent idea. In this part of the chapter, we will be trying to point out ways in which stoic practices might have a certain level of value in assisting positive psychology to help people achieve moral virtue as well as enhancing general well-being in people.

Positive psychologists carried out literature research on virtues and consequently came up with six virtues that included the four fundamentals virtues of contemporary Greece- courage, justice, wisdom, and self-control. Nonetheless, while stoics, as well as other Roman and Greek, were mostly convinced that all these virtues were necessary for somebody to lead a better life, specialists in positive psychology, alternatively sell the idea that people should work on finding their strengths and in turn use the newly found strength to improve their senses or feeling of well-being. Strengths are more direct, operationalized forms of virtues. For example, wisdom as a virtue has been split into strengths like curiosity, creativity, love of perspective and learning and judgment. There is almost indisputable evidence that using somebody's strength in new ways revamps somebody is feeling of well-being. However, it is still unclear whether this is the best way to make somebody virtuous. An argument has ensued with the suggestion that virtue may need the opposite, which basically gives more attention to the moral standards that somebody lacks. For instance, if a woman is courageous but she does not have self-control, should she continue exhibiting her courage or should she work on improving her self-control?

Better still, it is more questionable whether they can really showcase, courage and self-control without being wise. Socrates once argued that opting to retreat could be more of an act of courage than attacking, depending on the situation. This is where wisdom comes in handy because it is required to determine which action was more virtuous.

Stoicism being a philosophy that is virtue-based, it is very suitable to take up the empty slots in positive psychology. Stoicism is of the idea that people should work on developing virtues in as much as they are not their strengths and provides them with the necessary exercises to give them a boost in doing so. By encouraging people to worry only about things that they have control over and being concerned with how other people are doing, stoic practices can help people in becoming wise. Stoic practices give psychology as well as the individual the chance to work on building their character as well as their well-being.

Is positive psychology the new stoicism?

To some extent, it would feel like history is trying to repeat itself. Stoic practices through direct or indirect channels tend to be seeing a subtle but significant reawakening off late. However, it would seem like stoicism has a new adversary, probably even presenting itself in disguise as a helper or defender. In as much as positive psychology has been instrumental in bringing us a series of character strengths, most of which are in line with classical, virtues, it appears to go off in a subtly opposite direction. This way it reminisces rivalries in the ancient times between Epicureanism, Astotelianism among others. The movement that flies the banner of positive psychology seems to have come up with yet a separate method to achieving the subjective goal of happiness. Is this not what all the schools of philosophy were looking for?

Simply put, the answer is No. What most primeval schools sought was the most trusted gateway to flourishing. This simply means having the ability to integrate fully and express the true nature of somebody in view of nature. Therefore, positive psychology brings flow on board but then again flow has no relation to flourishing whatsoever.

Therefore, we will attempt to sort out the setback of the positive psychology approach and then the practicable stoic response.

The question of whether the activity you constantly immerse yourself in is worthwhile? Is it helpful to you and to the world? The stoic's response would be based on examining a certain activity against 'oikeiosis'. Does this activity benefit my preservation as an individual and flourishing as a rational and physical being? Are its effects the same on the people that I am responsible for and whom I am related to via normal societal bonds, species or even life in general? If it results in improved sustainability, improvement or expansion of the circles of supremacy, then chances are that the value of the activity will be high.

On the question of talent. Whether you are extremely good at what you do or you are simply wasting time

The stoic creation of 'phusis' that is normally understood in its cosmos form assists us in directing our thoughts and focus in this regard. Phusis goes beyond the natural existence of animals and plants. Phusis encourages us to not only live in peace and according to the natural domain but to wake up and explore our individual phusis. The abilities and talents that are waiting to be grabbed by us so that we can express and improve them. Simply put, the whole idea of going through fulfillment is so that we can fulfill the promise of nature. Our nature.

The question about balance. Are you supposed to spend your time going after the moments of flow or there is more to be said in regard ensuring that you balance the gift you possess with our exploits like building relationships and love?
In the case of the stoic, the only authentic 'end' that people should go after is the status of 'eudemonia', that refers to a condition of flourishing, and that the only gateway to

Eudaimonia is practicing virtue towards goals that are appropriate. The Stoics came up with five reactions or approaches to the somebody is likely to through in life as he/she seeks to fulfill his/ her roles and responsibilities

We are supposed to go after the things that preserve us or promote us as reasonable human beings. Thereafter we may choose to pursue those things that preserve and promote us as physical beings. We should strive to remain in a neutral state to the things that have no rational or physical impact on us. Nonetheless, we should be on the watch out for things that aim at breaking the physical being in us. We should categorically reject anything that poses a danger to the rational beings in us.

In as much as positive psychology appears to sound the correct notes, the playing tune is entirely modern. In as much as it appears to have acquired themes from the symphony of stoicism, it has cut the pursuit for the so-called good life. If stoicism is correctly understood, rigorously practiced, realistically applied, it will result in a lot of balance and life worth.

Chapter 4: The Power of Thinking Bigger Than Yourself

Back then, before I understood Stoicism and its philosophers, I did not know the meaning of life. However, after learning and getting knowledge on some of the principles of great Stoics like Marcus Aurelius and Seneca, I was able to give myself to a greater cause than me. Right now I can tell you to find the nearest charitable organization to work as a volunteer. I can also tell you to give up your time to service.

However, all these that I tell you will make no sense unless I also tell you the value of being a part of something is not about you. It is in us as humans that at times we tend to feel incapable and tend to hold on to what we have. As humans, there are times that we usually think and contemplate about the loss of our life at one point in time. Well, it is also reasonable to consider forfeiture of all that we possess. In the same way, a day shall come when you and the close things that you hold dear will depart, so will you and your goods, assets, and chattels. Whatever secular law says or whatever you might, think about your children, pension, portfolio or house, in a fundamental sense these things are not yours; they are just temporary gifts that will be gone one day. Stoics, therefore, teach that the above point implies that humans should regard themselves as stewards rather than owners of wealth. Non-stoic will often think about what they want but do not have or cannot have. For Stoics, Marcus Aurelius advised that we should learn to appreciate what we possess now and try to think how much we would miss what we have if they were taken away from us. In this way, we will learn to appreciate what we have. Seneca on the Happy Life exhorts us to celebrate life. However, he also cautions that we should not develop much love for the things that we enjoy. We should not be slaves of the gifts of Fortune.

The power of thinking bigger than yourself begins by knowing yourself. Philosopher Socrates in his philosophical teachings once said that the unexamined life is a life not worth living. When Socrates was asked to give a summary of all philosophical commandments, his reply was simple: "Know yourself." Humans are destined for far more than just mere survival. Lending from Socrates' philosophical teachings, knowing oneself has an extraordinary prestige among the Stoics. This is the meaning of life. Therefore, you have to ask yourself why self-knowledge is such a prestigious good. What are the things you are likely to experience when you lack self-knowledge? What should we do to know ourselves? How do we come to learn such things? Why is difficult to attain self-knowledge? From these questions, it is clear that there are a million things that we can potentially know about ourselves. The reason why self-knowledge matters is that it plays one central role: It offers us a path to knowing ourselves thus greater fulfillment and happiness. By lacking self-knowledge, you become vulnerable to mistaken ambitions and accidents. When we have the right sort of self-knowledge, by greater chances, we can avoid errors in whatever we are dealing with and thus we will be able to formulate our life choices.

The ability to think bigger than yourself is the key to extreme success. But wait. What does it mean to think bigger than yourself? Thinking bigger than yourself relates to the ability of an individual to be able to dream and visualize what he/she can achieve without putting any limits on his/her thinking. Thinking bigger than yourself is all about having an open mind that can see things more positively and creatively and be able to as well see opportunities in the big picture. One of the Tony Robins quotes I find to be interesting is where he says that the moment you have mastered time, you will be able to have an understanding and clear view of how most people tend to overestimate their accomplishments in a year and as well underestimate what they can achieve in a decade.

If we underestimate what we can achieve in the long term, then we are underestimating our true capabilities. In other words, we are simply lowering our goals to what we can term as "achievable" levels. Because we can easily meet the "achievable" levels, we lower generally lower our expectations, we lower our standards and we lower our outcomes.

Look through and see some of the people you can identify as successful and with good personal virtues; surely one thing you will realize is that they avoid this thinking. They instead challenge themselves by setting big goals. Naturally, we can achieve more and even get further within a shorter time the moment we are ready to stretch for something rather than coasting towards that thing. When we have bigger goals, even the things that may seem to slow us down will be of less importance. When we have bigger goals, we become swifter in providing solutions to issues that may hinder us from achieving our goals. The human mind is a very powerful tool and can automatically prioritize the things that are important if the goal is well big and defined. Thinking bigger than you can motivate your thoughts and actions. Here are the ways with which you can think bigger than yourself;

i.   Be Positive And Fearless

Fearful or negative thoughts will lead you to small thinking. In all your thoughts, eliminate the word impossible and instead, come up with the reasons as to why you 'can'. You can also find the reasons why you think that you cannot. Regardless of the approach you take, just ensure that you become a self-fulfilling prophecy. Thinking beyond yourself requires that you be able to see problems in the form of challenges and challenges as opportunities. Thinking bigger than yourself will help you to create unlimited solutions, possibilities, and alternatives. Turn your attention to being optimistic, brave and bold.

ii. Visualize Without Restraint

It is the lack of resourcefulness and not resources that hold people back. Being able to think bigger than you mean that you have to visualize future possibilities rather than just being stuck in the present. Develop in you the critical thoughts on how to look at things not as they are now but rather how they can be when there are no constraints. By simply visualizing your thoughts, you provide value to everything in your thoughts. Visualizing gives you a compelling taste giving you clarifications on how your vision will be when turned to reality. This makes you feel motivated to make it happen. This will make you come up with creative solutions towards realizing your goals.

iii. Ask Big Questions

More often, practice asking yourself and others bigger and more challenging questions. For instance, you can ask yourself the following questions;

- If you were given a chance to change one thing about the world, what would you prefer to change?
- Which people or who do you think will benefit most from what you know?
- What would you do if you had an unlimited supply of money?

- If you would be turned to be immortal, what would you do?

Great leaders are people who spend much of their time seeking advice and asking lots of questions. They do not give more advice and answering questions. Feedbacks coming from other people regarding your big questions are very valuable in shaping thoughts on such issues.

iv.   Be Creative And Always Dream Big

It is good that you go big. Remember that the size of your success is determined by the size of your belief. Without censorship, do some creative brainstorming. Think of how you can develop your big dreams into a reality. Imagination is the key to success. Let your ideas flow freely, give yourself time to dream and while imagining and dreaming, take note of the greatest ideas. From there, concentrate on that idea never giving up on until your vision becomes a reality. Create a vision in you that is very inspirational and that can ignite the fire within you. In this way, you will be able to commit and feel excited when working towards that dream.

v.   Set Bigger Long-Term Goal And Stick To This Goal

Decide on something big (a big long-term goal) and give it all your focus towards achieving this goal. Ensure that your attention is turned to what you want and be the person to make it happen. In whatever we always focus on and whatever we take action on, we will always get it. To be a successful person, you must be ready to do anything and everything you can just to achieve your goals.

vi.   Always Inspire Those Around You

Successful people are those who connect with others. Thinking bigger than yourself will give you confidence which will, in turn, attract others. Therefore, use these qualities to see that you bring others onside. Once you develop the ability to inspire and leverage others you will be able to bring more people on board. When you think big, it means that you have big ideas. Big ides not only motivate the people around you but also inspires them. This is the only way to easily attract and build a following in this highly connected world where this seems to be very difficult. Today, we advantaged that we have social networks. You can use social media to quickly spread your big ideas and gain resources needed for making your ideas a reality. Ensure that you leverage on the people around you as this is also one of the best ways of making your ideas turn to reality.

Take action. You can start eating the elephant bit by bit and one bite at a time. Goals are just dreams that you have captures and pinned them down and now you have planned the actions for achieving these goals. When you follow through your plan by action, you will succeed. On a daily basis, ensure that you take steps towards achieving your big goal even if it means spending only 15 minutes per day. This will play a great role in achieving your long-term big goal.

vii.   Believe In Yourself Above Anything Else

Believing in yourself is very important in achieving greatness. When you believe that it can happen, then it can happen. Ensure that you magnify your thinking power. The moment you learn that life is much broader and that everything that exists around you was not made by people who were not smatter than you, you actually make yourself aware that you are able to change or influence in these things. It also means that you are also able to build things that other people can use. The moment you teach yourself this fact, you will never be the same. Therefore, be confident and put it in your mind that you can do it and nothing will stop you.

At any moment, never underestimate the power of your thoughts. Consistently make your thoughts even bigger. One fact about the inventions we see today is that they all started with big ideas and with people who were able to think bigger than themselves. It is only big thinkers who can change the world. Big thinkers are today's leaders, they are the today's achievers and innovators. And this is because they have freed their minds from small thinking and limitations. By thinking big, you are moving towards having a more widened horizons and this is what will take you out of the ordinary and direct you into the extraordinary.

As a big thinker, practice putting your thoughts not only into effect but also into actions. There should be no limit on the realization of your goals. Consistently go for the bigger and better. Cultivate a culture in you that gives you the zeal, energy and drive towards seeing your dreams into a reality. The higher you aim, the bigger your goals, the higher you will go, the bigger you will achieve. Expand your thinking, expand your mind and expand all your horizons.

Chapter 5: Practice Objectivity

Stoicism right from its origin divides the philosophical discourse into three main categories; "Ethics," "Physics" and "Logic." How can we practice the Stoic practical disciplines? The answer to this lies in practicing objectivity. Stoicism teaches you how to develop and have a calm life and a rational mind regardless of happening around you. In other words, Stoicism helps you to have a focus and an understanding of what your mind can control and therefore have no worry about what about you as well accept the things that you cannot control. Let us have a look at how to practice objectivity in Stoicism.

Learn To Live In Agreement With Nature

Living in agreement with nature is the stoic goal/purpose of life. It is somehow challenging to translate this goal of life. Man is the only rational animal and our ability to reason differentiates us from the rest of the other animals. For better and worse reasons, man is different and dominates all other species found on the planet. Therefore, our point of interest as humans should therefore not be on the fact that we have different skin or smaller teeth but should rather be on our mental and social abilities. Our capacity for rationality is what distinguishes us from the rest of all other species. That is the reason why there are times that you will hear people say "don't behave like a sheep" or "don't be an animal." In other words, this means that as humans, our ability to apply to reason in any way that we action means a lot. The moment we use our reasoning ability, then we live a life that is in agreement with what nature dictates because that makes us act the way we were meant to. As humans, we are not required to act like animals but rather we should apply reason in order to act like humans. Applying reason brings us to another goal of life, which is living in accordance with virtue.

Live By Virtue

Living by virtue is the highest of all goods. When you are able to live according to virtue, then you are probably living the Good Life. In Stoicism, virtue is classified under three main categories referred to as the four cardinal virtues.

i.   Prudence/Wisdom: Under this category, humans should practice good judgment, excellent deliberation, and good sense.

ii. Justice or Fairness: Under this category, a man should be able to portray benevolence, fair dealing, having a heart, and effective public service.

iii. Courage: These virtues are confidence, bravery, perseverance, and honesty.

iv. Self-Discipline: Under this virtue category, an individual should be orderly, practice self-control, being humble, forgiveness.

When you can act according to these virtues, under Stoicism, you are considered to be progressing towards Eudemonia (the Good Life) which the main goal of life. Therefore, living the Good Life depends on two main things; living according to virtue and perfection of reason. Under the teachings of Stoicism, you can only be considered to be virtuous if and only if you practice all the above mention virtues. For instance, if you are a man with good judgment, fair dealing, and confidence but still practice binge drinking, you are not truly virtuous. When you get involved in binge drinking, you break one of the virtues of self-discipline. Virtue by itself is its own reward. When you take a particular action, do it because that action is the right thing to be done. When you take an action, ensure that whatever you are doing agrees with what nature dictates and is in accordance with the four cardinal virtues. What you get out of this action doesn't matter because by simply acting according to the four virtues, the self-reward of these four virtues is enough since this means that you are clearly progressing towards having the Good Life.

It is the responsibility of human beings to do what is right. Concerning this, we can also define virtue as excelling in your personal characters and the application of the power of reason in a healthy and praiseworthy way. In Stoicism, what matters are your actions and characters? There are also situations whereby acting according to virtue can bring further benefits. For example, you are an individual love technology and the innovations involved with it. You decide to catch a bus on your way home. However, you find yourself alone in the back seat and next to you, there is a phone, seemingly someone forgot it or it dropped from his/her pocket. You check through the phone and you realize that it cannot be tracked. You remember that you are currently using some second-hand with minimize features and this is because your phone was recently stolen at some live concert. This seems to be a win-win situation. However, based on the virtues in you, you reason out that it is appropriate you should return. You, therefore, decide to call one person on the contact list and eventually you meet the owner of the phone. The owner gets very excited and even decides that you should have some coffee. Well, this will make you happy. In Stoicism, these benefits are interpreted as an added bonus. However, the primary motive behind taking such action should not be driven by the desire to get these benefits.

It is appropriate that you always involve reasoning and as well try to do the right thing. Your actions should be guided by the virtues of self-discipline, wisdom, courage, and justice. The yields of our virtuous actions are not entirely up to us and thus the results behind your actions should be based on the benefit. Focus on the things that you can control, which excellently defines you in terms of character.

Differentiate What Is Good from what is Bad As Well as Indifferent Things

Stoicism differentiates what is good from what is bad and these two from Preferred/unpreferred indifferent things. According to Stoics, what we consider as good are the four virtues requiring us to have self-discipline, to be wise, be courageous and be just in all our dealings. On the other hand, bad things are things that are in opposition to the four cardinal virtues which include indulgence, folly, injustice, and cowardice. Lastly, indifferent things are things like life and death, good health and poor health, pleasure and pain, fame and bad reputation and wealth and poverty. In other words, we can summarize indifferent things basing on three main categories which are wealth, health and reputation. It is quite interesting that Stoic indifferent things are reflected exactly the things that are used today by ordinary people to judge good and bad.

However, Stoics believe that as rational beings, the indifferent things cannot harm or help our flourishing. They have no role in the Good Life. This, therefore, means that indifferent things (reputation, wealth and health) differ completely to the Good Life and simply are of no importance. We cannot say that the indifferent thing is good or bad because they are indifferent. Your ultimate happiness does not rely on whether you are poor or rich. It is appropriate that we not only learn how we can be indifferent particularly towards things considered as indifferent but also learn how to gain satisfaction with anything that nature provides us with.

We should never substitute indifference for coldness. This is often a misconception that makes Stoics to be looked at as unemotional people. This statement on its own seems to be self-contradicting because when asked, for instance, is it right to say that being of good health is all ways better than being of poor health. The answer we will all agree on is yes. This is because there are indifferent things that are very valuable when compared to others. Therefore, philosophers had to provide a distinction between good and bad in different things which they ended naming them as; (1) preferred in different things and (2) dispreferred indifferent things. Looking at the differentiation of the indifferent things from a Stoic logical point of view, positive indifferent things include good things like good health, good looks, wealth, friendship and a good reputation. The opposite of these good things was the dispreferred indifferent. This now makes sense, right? However, Stoics further made clarity on the differentiation of indifferent things. Stoics explained that regardless of our social status, looks, wealth or health, our ultimate goal is to live the Good Life. Although all these are the preferred qualities, they remain to be indifferent and as such, they are not really necessary to have in order to achieve a virtuous life.

As humans, we tend to prefer to be wealthy and not poor, to have good health and not to be sick, to be happy and not sad. Stoics allowed that you can proceed to search for these things but note that when searching, do in accordance with virtue because, without virtue, your integrity is endangered. What we mean is that it is better for one to endure poverty, sickness or pain in a way that is considered as honorable as to search for health, wealth or joy in a manner that is rather shameful.

For Example

Under different things, we will look at friendship as a preferred indifference. Generally, it is good for us to have people close to us (friends) than not to have such people (friends). Stoics, however, would rather choose virtue over friendship when told to make a decision regarding the two. Therefore, a Stoic will not lie in order to save a friend. To Stoics, that would mean neglecting morality and thus justice will weigh more than friendship. Character and morality are greater than friendship and love.

Take Action

As the saying goes, a true philosopher is a warrior of his/her mind. Even though most of the things are not within our control, you can still find something about your own life. You can't just lay back and so nothing. This does not work for Stoics.

Regardless of what we do, we can never determine the way events should happen. We can rather determine the happening of events along with what we do because the outcomes of events will often depend on our actions. You will never get the Good Life when you simply lie down and relax doing nothing. This will never make you a good person. The Good Life is only earned by taking the right actions.

Our satisfaction on how to live life should not just come from the learning of abstract ideas but should rather come from the vigorous application of those ideas. Knowledge and talks are two useless and cheap things when not applied. Therefore, given that we do not put into action what we learn, then we will, in the end, do what is opposite. In ancient times, a true philosopher was seen as an individual with brilliance and that loves wisdom. In the pursuit of self-mastery, a true philosopher wins the battles in his/her own mind and goes out into practicing his/her philosophical thoughts. This is different from what we see today. Most of the philosophers today are much more like librarians of the mind. They simply accumulate ideas and theoretical knowledge in their brain. They forget that the most important this is to live the ideas.

Chapter 6: Living According to Nature

Every Stoic thinker believes in the motto: "living according to nature." In his meditations, Marcus Aurelius, the Stoic Emperor explained this belief by saying that "Philosophy will only require what your nature already demands." Zeno, the founder of Stoicism on the other defined nature as "the way things work" and thus it only requires wisdom to act in accordance with natural laws. Seneca, another Stoic, explains that "as humans, we need to keep to the way which Nature has mapped out for us. If humans follow Nature, everything will be easy and unobstructed. However, if we combat Nature, then there is no difference between us and those men ho row against the current." In other words, all these thoughts from Emperor Marcus Aurelius, Zeno, and Seneca make us conclude that "live according to nature" is probably the motto of the Stoic School.

Well, for any reader who picks up Stoicism, I know this definitely sounds strange. However, the Stoic prescription believes that human nature is impulsive and selfish. Therefore, what the Stoics had in mind was generally above the natural base impulses seen in normal humans. The greatest gift that nature ever gave humans was the power to reason and this is what separated humans from the unthinking animals. Here are the Stoic rules that will help and guide you to live according to nature.

Give Focus to What Is Within Your Power

It is only by first accepting our natural limitations (both inherent and circumstantial limitations) that can we live according to nature. The laws that govern life and nature, whether good or bad, cannot be changed by humans. In any case that we want to live lives free from disturbance, we should quickly accept this fact. Freedom can only come once we understand the limits of our power as humans and the natural limits that the divine provisions have set in place. The moment we accept the limits and inevitabilities in our lives; we become able to learn how to work with these limits and inevitabilities rather than fighting them. By doing so, we become free.

Therefore, assess yourself, your thoughts and feelings to have a better understanding of your talents and natural affinities. Build on what you are and ensure that you make most of it. Never strive for things that are completely beyond your present capacities because this will end up making you frustrated. When a man is in harmony with himself, the man pursues limited natural desires. The desire for more (greed) which the Stoic describes as not being natural cannot be satisfied. This means that if you are an individual seeking things that are outside your control for instance, things like wealth, physical pleasure or reputation, you will definitely end up a very frustrated person. Seneca talks about this by pointing out that poverty and wealth are all relative concepts. When a man chooses to restrain himself within the bounds set by nature, such a man will not notice poverty. However, when a man exceeds the bounds set by nature, such a man will be pursued by poverty regardless of how rich such a man may be.

Philosophy Is A Way of Life

We are encouraged by philosopher Epictetus to always have courage in approaching our daily activities with the same degree of seriousness and discipline displayed by soldiers or singers during their training. Regardless of whether a matter is small and domestic or grand and public, always conduct yourself in accordance with the laws of nature. Your utmost deal should always ensure that you harmonize your will with nature. Practice this ideal in your own daily life and in your personal tasks and duties. Aristotle believes that your virtue is defined by your habit and not an isolated act. The best way for one to absorb Stoic principles can only be through good habits. Both desire and aversion can be considered as powerful habits. However, we have the capability to train ourselves to develop and have better habits.

Avoid habits that give you the desire to pursue things that are not within your control. We should also instead focus on combatting the things that are not good for us and are within our power. Every individual has his/her own weaknesses and inclinations. The most effective way we can use to counter character flaws is by opposing such characters with contrary habits. Just the same, way we devote ourselves to fear pain or excessively to physical pleasure, we should also train ourselves in the opposite extremes of what we love.

Demonstrate Absolute Commitment to Truth

When you choose to live according to the requirements of nature, be ready to be absolutely committed to truth. There is nothing good that will ever come from superstitious beliefs, fear, wishful thinking or greed. The worst of all things you can do is lying to yourself. Lying to yourself will separate you from your natural instincts. This is what results in a sense of disconnectedness. The Stoic teaches that we need to develop in us an attitude of complete honesty especially to oneself. Absolute commitment to truth means that in every thought, every word/utterance, and in every life moment.

Open your eyes and learn to see things for what they really are as this will spare you from the pain caused by avoidable devastation and false attachments. Regardless of how we perceive people and things or how they appear to us, the fact is that they will remain what they are. Therefore, instead of diverting our eyes from the painful events in our lives, we need to look at them properly and then think about these events often. When we face the real events caused by disappointments, death or infirmity, we free ourselves from the illusions and false hopes. In this way, we avoid being miserable or envious thoughts.

View Adversity as both a Challenge and an Opportunity

Adversity tests the honesty we have to ourselves. We have to face adversity because it is part of nature. You will be considered as ignorant of one half of nature if you claim to be always fortunate that you have never passed through a life that has never known sorrow. Through adversity, we discover our mettle. We should accept the challenges that are posed by misfortunes. When we are faced with difficulties in life, we are presented with the opportunity to turn to our inner being and invoke the submerged inner resources in us. We can only be able to know our strengths from the trials we endure.

Chapter 7: The Science of Letting go of the Past and Live in the Present Moment

Let go of the past by stopping any attachment you have with painful memories. The memories may be dragging you back without your knowledge. Forget about your past pains, and you start accepting what the future has in store for you. You need to fight the past and not letting discouragement or disappointment bring you down. Move on with life and make things sail away as they should. Release the thoughts that are build up in you, habits, fears as well as worries. Detach yourself from the past emotions that make you resentful so that you can face the future an active person. If you do not let go of the past, you will suffer bad relations, jealous as well as envy. Letting go needs you to have a determination and work daily on your life.

There are things that you can involve in your daily practice so that you can leave that past behind and have a good future. They include and not limited to;

Making Peace with the Past

It is time that you agree that what happened at that time belongs to the past and not the future. Do not let that bring you down or tie you to an extent you cannot live a healthy future. Thinking about the bad things that have gone will not help you in any way. That will do you more harm than good. Though your mind will keep bringing back the painful memories, you need to replace them with positive ones with immediate effect. Be smart and creative to counter any negative thought that wants to remind you about what you did in the past. Teach your mind to think about a positive tomorrow when the past tries to haunt you. That will in no time become a habit, and you will eventually find yourself letting go of the range you have. You can practice mindfulness as a technique to replace the negative thoughts. When you bring your focus to the present, the past will have a lesser impact on your future. Practice living the present, and you will be hurt less and as well be in a position to control the hurt. You are free to choose the things you want in life, and you have to make a wise decision so that you can live the life of your expectations.

Face your Fears

Fear can be the thing that is holding you back from letting go of your past. To continue with a healthy life, you have to face your concerns as well as disappointment. Cut your connection with the fears, and you will make it in life. You have to keep trying, and eventually, you will make it. People will often have a fear of being in grief, sadness, anger, as well as disappointment. Do not shut out such feelings; instead, give them a chance to flow out of you. When you decide to fight them, you will be left stuck, and you will find it hard to move on. Do not avoid the negative emotions from the past since that will make you dwell in the past. Naturally, a person will find a means to counter any pain that will come their way. Spending most of your time trying to distract your feeling will not initiate a disconnection. Finding something which you like doing so that you will take your mind off the past will yield no fruits. You need to know that the more you do that, the more you will get hurt. Focusing on such things will only drain your energy. When you feel as if you cannot do it on your own, find someone you think will help you get over the past.

Practice Being Gentle with Yourself

Show yourself some compassion as well as kindness so that the past can stop tormenting you. Do not criticize yourself when you get in a painful situation. Treat yourself in the same way you would treat the person you love. If you do not love yourself, you will have a hard time fighting with the past, and that means that your future will be full of bruises. Even though the hurt is in no way inevitable, treat yourself with at most love as well as a kindness if it will come. Practice self-care once you are hurt, and that will be a way of setting clear boundaries. Say no to the things that harm you and do the things that bring you joy as well as comfort you not forgetting to handle your needs first. When you learn to implement self-care daily, you will empower yourself, and there will be an overwhelming feeling. Put all the focus on yourself and address the resentment build up in you. Try and bring yourself to the present any time that you feel that your thoughts the drifting t the past. Pay attention to the things that you are grateful for and not what hurts you.

Do not wait for an Apology

You know you are firm when you accept an apology from someone who has wronged you, and they do not apologize. Expecting someone to apologize is the worst mistake that you will ever make. That will make you go slow in letting the past go and, in most cases,, is when that person does not care what happens to your future. Do not expect them to take care of your healing: instead, you should take care of your healing process. The pain, as well as hurt that is build up in you not affect the person who hurt you, but they are on you. Do not wait for the person to make an apology and keep in mind that they will not apologize. When you do that, you will speed up your healing, and the quicker you will let go. Work on your forgiveness since waiting for them to apologize will stall the entire process. Forgiveness is an essential thing to do since it will relieve you from the shame, anger, sadness as well as the guilt that is in you.

Be Free to Talk About It

When passing through the hard times, you should find someone that you can speak with them about it. When you speak it out, it will be one way to help you heal, and you will let it go. When you don't talk about it, you will never improve and dwelling in the past will make your life retard. Do not shame or feel as if it is embarrassing to talk about it to the people around you. Find someone who will be patient enough with you and willing to offer you the help they can get so that you can leave the past behind. You can as well sort for professional advice once you feel as if you have no one you can trust. When you talk to a therapist, the struggle to let go of will go decreasing, and finally, you will manage. When you come across a professional who has experience in such matters, they will guide you on how to implement the process.

Practice Mindfulness

Practicing mindfulness is a way to train the brain to live in the present and focus your awareness on the senses and not the thoughts. Focus your attention on the things that are happening at the moment. Leave alone what went on some time back and let it remain as history. Aim at noticing every activity that is and let the mind float without any attachment. Make it a practice, and you will get it easy to refocus your thoughts on what is going on in the present. Find a starting point and begin so that you can let go of the past. It may be a hard thing to do, but once you can practice that, you will find ideas flowing in the right direction.

Create a Distance

It will be of help to you if you create a gap between the person of the situation that is continually reminding you if the past. Whatever that is making, you upset should not be anywhere close to you. It is not a bad idea to put a physical distance from the person to who is making you dwell in your past. Create a psychological range as well from any circumstance that is taking you back to the past. You need to avoid anyone that is advising you that battling with the past will not help you in any way. No one should discourage you from processing the past since it will be an excellent approach to use so that you can heal.

Be Creative

Creativity when it comes to real life is a way to let go of your past. When you engage your mind in creating new beginnings as well as things, you will have less time to dwell in the past. Open up your thoughts to new opportunities and do the things that will make you happy. Seek to meet new people when the ones who are with you discourage you from moving in that direction. You need to embrace change whenever it comes your way. Take a different course and guidance when things seem to make a change. It will work for you since change is as good as rest. Yearn to discover more, and that will help you to let go of the anger that you feel in you due to your past mistakes.

Work with a Positive Attitude

You need to create affirmative phrases that you need to keep reminding yourself once the painful past tries to find a way in you. The way you talk to yourself will determine whether you will move forward or you will still keep moving steps backward. The more you talk positivity about yourself, the more you can leave the past behind. You can reframe your mind often when you practice a mantra that you will be telling yourself when you are in a painful as well as an emotional moment. Train your mind to think about the possible and not the impossible. In that way, you will move forward more efficiently and forget how the future was treating you. Bring the people that see the good in you closer. You need to as well focus on your strengths rather than your weaknesses.

You need to know that both the positive and the negative experiences will help shape the future. You will come across people, situations as well as events that will determine who you will be in the days to come. Be wise that you will not focus on the negative ones and the ones that will bring you to hurt. That will help you overcome any experience that will be similar to the one in the past. And you will not be biased. You will be hit by mental blindness in the future when you decide to focus on the negative side alone. Spending all your time in fighting impossibility at the moment will tie your spiritual resources, keeping you away from a good life. You will make a difference with the way you are going to deal with the painful past. Bear in mind that emotional pain will keep you away from healing.

You need to simplify your life so that the unforeseen consequences will not hit you. Living in the past will only rob your present joy. Choose to live in the future, and you will find it exciting and have a healthy and meaningful life. Live in the present moment, and the future will have a smooth flow. When you learn how to let go of the past, seek to know how you need to live. Focus on living in the present. Leaving the past behind is not only an important thing but living the resent is a wise decision to make. Mourning the past will make you worry about the present as well as the future. It will make you always anticipate troubles, and you will have it hard to cope with life. Aim for the best, and you are going to find it enjoyable living in the present moment. Make a conscious decision and be in control of every situation celebrating every small achievement that you make.

Chapter 8: Easy Steps to Become Unattached to External Things

Detaching yourself is healthy, especially when it involves going away from toxic people. You will benefit if you disconnect from things that do not help you. Separating is a practice that should be done once you find yourself in entanglements that drag you behind. Find happiness as you disconnect yourself from unhealthy attachments using the following approaches.

Know the Reason You Want To Detach

Know why you need to disconnect from the attachments you have been thinking they are a hindrance to your success. Ask yourself in what way you are going to do it and the appropriate time to start the process. It will be hard for you to do it if you have enough reason to do that. As you seek to detach yourself, have a concrete goal that you are clinging on. The aim must be convincing to you why you need to leave a particular thing. The reason will be the one to help you each day to stay firm to disconnect yourself slowly. The goal should not stop once you get to some point in your journey. The reason should help you realize yourself even when you feel like there is no more hope. It should have a direct connection with the thing or person you intend to detach. Find the exact cause and how it is affecting you as well as the people around you.

Release

Let the thing that is depriving your happiness go so that you can be at peace. It will be of great help if you let it go. The longer you keep holding on it, the more it will harden and hurt you, the more. You will end up blowing if you keep holding onto something that is not beneficial to you. Some things are toxic, and they need to be left alone. Do the things that you know will help you to let them go. You can even decide to pen down the thoughts that are pissing you off and analyze one by one and how to go about them. When you need to let go of a person, at times you might find yourself crying. If that is the only way feel that can make you release them, then you can go ahead and do it. When you learn to release someone or something, you will find the attachment you were having declining slowly with time. There are numerous ways that you can release something, but you have to make sure it will be harmless. Decide the amount of time that you will use to let go, but you should not take an eternity. The approach that will make you remain calm is the best option to use. Your harmony is the most important thing above everything else. It is all about you and the feeling that comes along with your attachment to that particular thing. Our opinions are what makes us the people we are, and no one should judge you for the way you feel.

Do it Little by Little

You do not have to load yourself, all you have to do is start small, and finally, you will manage to break the attachment. Time is all that you need to perform a big task. Do not shock yourself but instead try harder and as days go by, you will detach completely. It is not easy, but eventually, it will be possible. It is painful to detach from something or someone close to you, but if they are of no gain, you have no choice but initiate a detachment. Start with removing anything that will be a constant reminder of them. You have the right to decide what you will start by eliminating. You may feel that you cannot let some things off the hook, but it is time you earn that holding on them will not help. Do not push too hard to the extent that you will tire before you are through with the entire process. When you do that, you might lose the focus and forget what you were aiming for. You will be forced to start from the first step when you lose the reason why you are pushing for the detachment.

Seek as well as Look Forward

Look for help as you seek a new start and living a new life. You need to have something that you are focusing on. That will serve as a motivator of going on with the process daily. As you are slowly letting go, you need to find a new thing that will always remind you that you have to keep holding on. Something to tell you that you have a better future ahead away from whatever that is distracting you. Do not dwell on pain that you felt in the past but fix your eyes on a better tomorrow. There is a sweet tomorrow before you, and that is what should motivate you to keep fighting. Imagine the joy that you will have once you manage to draw away the external things that are holding your success. Let the imaginations that you have the fuel you to detach as fast as you can. Do not let anyone whisper defeat because if you give the surrounding a chance to drive you, you will eventually give up. Stay positive on whatever the outcome will be, and you will find satisfaction in the whole process. As you seek something exciting, look forward to great results.

Do not take Shortcuts

Detaching from something will take time, and for that, you need to have a lot of patience. There are no alternative routes to use, and you have to follow the right channel so that you can get to the results you desire. There has never been an easy way to detach from something that you have been with for some time. It turns out to be difficult and painful as well. But with the time, you will realize that there is no much pain than holding on to someone or something that you are not worth fighting. You have to take heart and be active as you detach yourself and start the journey of reinventing yourself.

Think forward and do not Look Back

There are no chances for you to pull back from the journey that you are set on. All the steps that you have gone through are essential, and you cannot lose focus at this juncture. When you think of looking back, you will be killing yourself slowly, and that will mean all has been in vain. When you look back from where you started it all, you will have more reasons to give up than to continue pushing. Despite there being many reasons to give up, pushing on will result in your freedom at the end of the tough journey of detaching. When you look back, you find things that will distract you from what the present, as well as the future, has for you in-store. You will not move any further when you get used to looking back. The past could be having sweet memories, but they are things that you cannot keep holding on that are from the past. They may be holding secrets that are tormenting as well as fears that are not necessary. Do not give up your future because of the history that you do not want to let go of. You should always be thinking of good things that are about to happen once you get away from some things. You can end up having better as well as healthier attachments once you let go of the unnecessary ones. You will be a better and happy person in the end. Have a determination to achieve what is before you rather than what you already have.

Learn to Forgive and Forget

Forgiving is a vital thing when you want to detach from things. Do not let pride take you over because that will harm the inner you. Give no chance for pride to win the battle since that is the number one thing that will destroy everything. Pride will make you say things that you will come to regret later. It will open up fresh wounds. Forgive yourself for having involved yourself in the things that hurt you and know that it is time to detach completely. Once you forgive, you will have a peace of mind and the strength to continue fighting. It will make you comfortable to know that there is nothing that is holding you back from detaching with toxic things and the environment. Forgiving may take quite some time, but it is much worth it. It will help you to separate with no traces of resentment in you. You not only have to forgive, but you need to put that in the past. You may not be in a position to forgive and forget, but you need to make sure that once you remember that situation, there will be no pain in you. Forgiveness will take you a step ahead when it comes to cutting the attachment that you had.

Healing

Wounds may take time to heal, but as time goes on, you will recover completely. The scars that you have maybe the reason why you want to disconnect so that you can heal. You can be in an attachment that is bringing you sorrow than joy. You have to cut the connection that there is so that you will stop suffering.

There comes a time that you feel your wounds are, and you wonder how you are going to heal. You need to detach yourself, and they will improve with time. Do not tear yourself apart so that you retain attachments that are bringing you scars. Try to heal for your sake and not for the others.

Always be Grateful

Appreciate the pain as well as the sorrow that you have. The memories that come along should be something to enjoy either good or bad. Be thankful that you have found a reason to end the attachment and move on. There are numerous things, as well as people, to be grateful. Detachment is a process, and it should be a reminder that you have to be happy without some things in life. Focus on the best side of issues, and you will have a reason to keep moving. Be grateful that the disconnection will give you a chance to look for healthier as well as beneficial attachments. You will have an opportunity to know your worth, and for that, you will learn to appreciate yourself.

Move Forward

The time that you have spent trying to detach yourself has been a success, and the next logical thing that you need to go is moving on with your life. Time has come for you to go forward without looking at what you have left behind. It is a chance to live a happy and healthy life away from toxic things. You have come to a great beginning, and you have to realize that and find your way forward. Coming back to your senses is the result of trying to find your worth. It is time to love the person you have become the way you should have done some time back. Face the world with courage and take one step at a time.

Life is a continuous cycle, and we can mess up along the way. That does not mean that we dwell on the toxic things and forget that we have a future ahead of us. We need to detach from some things so that we can have a life that is worth celebrating. There comes a time, and we feel as if we are not going to make it. Do not forget that there is a way out of every mess that you find yourself. Take the lessons that every attachment you are in teaches you so you can have a better tomorrow without dwelling in the past. When you feel as if you have cannot break the connection on your own, it will be good if you look for a professional to help you go through it. You will find it painful but the pain will not go forever.

Chapter 9: Controlling your Environment and Live in Complete Harmony

The world is full of issues that affect the way people lead their lives. There are trillions of issues that surround the environment over which people dwell. The aspect indicates that the context in which one lives has a direct impact on the art of being at peace. Thus, it is worth noting that if you don't take active steps to control your environment, there are chances that your situation will control the way you live and you may never have peace of mind within you. It is worth noting that the environment that surrounds an individual includes the food one eats, the places one sleeps, the clothes one wears, as well as the systems that surround an individual. It is worth noting that when one considers the food that one eats, there are chances that all of us understand the kind of food that one ought to eat. However, people are different as they choose to eat unhealthy foods that end up affecting their health as well. The aspect indicates that although one might be having a desire to lead a certain kind of life, the environment might have a significant impact on the behavior as well as the things that one does. However, if one can effectively control their setting, the aspect means that they will be in an excellent position to do what they feel is right and end up living in harmony with everything.

Take a look at some of the factors in the environment that ought to be controlled for one to live in harmony.

The Systems

The things that one does comprises of the systems that dictate the way one lives. The aspect includes the behaviors that cover our lives the climate as well as the places we live in. A noisy environment means that one won't be able to concentrate on petty issues. A noisy environment is distractive and encourages chaos.

In most cases, people make a lot of noise when in chaos or when they have differences. However, a cold environment indicates that one can effectively can and deliberate on sensitive issues. It is worth noting that a noisy environment or instead, a chaotic environment triggers a kick start of bad behaviors. It is worth noting that a pleasant climate triggers a kick start of healthful behaviors. The way human beings are created, the more one behaves well, the more a feeling of inner peace is created within an individual. Thus, if you live in a noisy environment, there are chances that you will be more involved in chaos and lack the inner peace that allows one to live in harmony. The other aspect worth noting is that the art of paying attention and remaining focused on the work is done will enable one to achieve more. In most cases, when one achieves the goals, there is an inner peace that is created within a person. Thus, creating a peaceful system is critical in increasing the art of leading in harmony.

The food

One of the most challenging aspects of life is eating healthy and leading a healthy life. The element is critical due to the fact that at times, people are engaged in activities where one learns on the things one ought to do to access some of these healthy foods and lead a healthy life. However, at times, one is not easy to access some of these foods. The aspect is linked to the fact that some are expensive, and not all individuals can afford such programmed eating habits. In most cases, the lack of proper feeding habits creates a specific environment within an individual. Also, the art of looking for food in different conditions or rather the art of struggling to secure a meal creates another environment that dictates the way a person lives.

It is worth noting that if you are ant struggling to secure a meal, the chances are that you will have peace of mind. In most cases, people who have peace of mind take tiny amounts of food, and they are satisfied. However, people who have real struggles before they secure a meal are never with an order with anyone. In most cases, they struggle to achieve food for their families as well as feeding themselves. Most of them end up working in very noisy or unconducive environments as they look for food.

In most cases, even after working for long hours, they don't have time to relax and enjoy life. The aspect is linked to the fact that they keep thinking of where they can secure a coin to buy meals that will never settle. They lack the peace of mind and are always working on trying and making ends meet. The realization that things aren't working for them creates more tension within such that they feel sad by life as well as the society at large. In most cases, such people are always bitter about the environment they live in. Some end up blaming others who might have led to them being in such situations. The aspect creates a negative atmosphere that doesn't foster harmony.

Bad Cues

It is worth noting that bad company corrupts good morals. In other words, if bad people or bad issues surround you, the chances are that you will start to behave as they do or be wrong as well. In other words, if you are surrounded by bad food, the chances are that it will begin to smell and you won't enjoy living in such an environment. In the same case, if you are involved in a company of bad people, you will end up behaving in the same way. It is worth noting that if one acts the opposite if the expectations, the society doesn't forget or forgive. In other words, if you work in a lousy manner, the community will hold the grudge as long as you live. Also, society may not be quick at understanding the reasons behind the actions done. Thus, even after selfo-justification, the corporation will remain in judgment.

Therefore, if the victim realizes that society is judging them, they won't be at peace and will never be able to lead a harmonious life.

Cleanliness

A clean environment is always safe and peaceful. In other words, if you live in a clean environment, you will be able to think right and do what is right. For instance, if you have terrible foods in a house, the chances are that they will start smelling bad once they go wrong. You can't live in such an environment and have peace.

In the same way, if you wear dirty clothes, the chances are that the guilt will kill you. In other words, you won't be a fee to interact with other people. There are chances that you will exclude yourself from the rest of society and looks for means of them noticing that you have dirty clothes. In most cases, your esteem will be lowered, and you won't be free in expressing what you think will work best for you.

It is also worth noting that a clean environment promotes one's health. In other words, there is no way you can stay in an unclean environment, eat from the same situation, and expect to lead a healthy life. Thus, the art of living healthy starts with the aspect of being clean and living in a clean environment. Therefore, as you develop the art of living healthy, you need to introduce cues that will encourage healthy living. Such signals include eating well and living in a clean environment. Leading a healthy life dictates some sense of peace within an individual. Thus, as you live, make a point of increasing the arty of positivity in your life by eating healthy and living in a calm environment and promote peace of mind within your life.

Exercises

Although society has not fully embraced the issues of exec rises, it is worth noting that the art of excises forms part of leading a healthy life. In other words, if you are used to frequent body exercises, the chances are that you will have reduced cases of complications, and you will develop diseases. The aspect indicates that you will not have time to cater to lifestyle diseases such as diabetes. In other words, you will live a holistic life free of sins. Thus, body exercises are part of the life that one ought to lead.

Controlling what enters the mind

As one lives, it is good to control what comes to your account. In most cases, it is g to have mindful thinking. Mindful thinking is rated as one of the best ways of cultivating a state of intense meditation known as dhyana. It is also rated as one of the best ways of relaxing. Also, the art of concentrating on one's breath has a positive effect on the entire mental and physical state of an individual.

The aspect of mindful thinking has four stages that allow one to think critically as he or she concentrates on breathing. In the first stage, one stay focused on the breath after breathing and counting one and tow, one breath out and repeat so for about ten minutes. In the second stage, one subtly shifts the inspiration and count as you breathe in and out. In the third stage, one is required to drop breathing and concentrate on watching the breath as it comes and goes. In the final step, one is expected to focus on concentration as it narrows and sharpens. At this point, you need to pay attention to the subtle sensation that occurs at the tip of your nose where the air passes.

The art of concentrating on one's breath allows one to remain focused on the mind as well. The accounts locate some time to relax and shed off some of the negative aspects of life that might have passed across. Mindful breathing is also helpful in the sense that it allows the mind to rest after critical thinking. It is also a crucial moment of offering the minds some room to feel or understand various aspect s of life. In other words, it is the best time to concentrate on how one partakes in different aspects of life.

It is worth noting that you can't have active meditation in a noisy environment. Also, a clean environment plays a critical role in fostering positive thinking, thus, as you plan to adjust to your situation so as you can think right, plan of making an environment that is safe, sound and clean. You may also color your averment with your best color to increase the arty of positivity.

I realize what works for you.

It is worth noting that various aspects of life are found in a particular environment. However, not all of them fit everyone. In other words, you might be living in a place where some different items or issues are available. It is critical to note that not all these items are useful. In words, you need to select the good things that fit you and make you feel good. There is no way you can find comfort in a car and expect to feel the same when the owner arrives.

In most cases, the mind's perception of an individual is affected by the environment that one lives in. Thus, as you select the food to eat, the clothes to wear as well as the places to sleep, you need to be sensitive and select those that fit you. The aspect is linked to the fact that if you are struggling to pay a particular bill of the place you are living, the chances are that you will not have a peace of mind. In most cases, you will be disturbed and quickly lose your art of concentration. Thus, losing a lot of energy as you try to fit in such an environment. Even the food that one's eats determined the effectiveness of an ecosystem. In most cases, the situation we are in determining the food we eat, the places one lives as well as the people one interacts with. The art creates some art of sense.

Chapter 10: The Best Way to Stay Focused On What You Can Control and Take Full Responsibility for Your Life

When you determine to focus on a better future, you will find it automatic that you are responsible for your daily life. You will not remain a loser, but you will be a victor. You will accept the fact that you are in charge of creating a better tomorrow than your today. You will learn to appreciate what will happen for you and not the one that will be happening to you. You are the one to determine how to respond to the changes that will occur in your life. You are the one who is responsible for the journey that you are about to start in your life. It will be of help to you if you will agree to be fully in charge of your life. There are approaches to use so that you will not lose your focus, and you stay in line with your goal. They include;

Eliminate distraction as well as time-wasters

When an emergency comes up, there is a need to deal with it there and then. Some of the things that come our way are not emergencies and do not require immediate action. Some of the situations will put themselves in order, and they do not have to distract us from our usual routine. When you respond to such cases, it will be a way to subject you to more issues. When you do not give a response, it will be a sign that you are an active person. There is nothing that will bother you when you can move time wasters on your way.

Remind yourself of what you are aiming

You need to find something that will keep telling you that you have a goal to hit. It will be a way to motivate you to keep moving on. You have full control of your life, and you do not have to waste time on something that is not beneficial to you. Take care of the things that you will invest your time in since you have a choice of how you will spend your time. Do not waste your time in something that is draining your energy. The things that will nourish you are what you should focus on. When you have the time to change your world, maximize that time to get the best out of it. Spend time in the things that will bring happiness in your life.

Live in the present

You do not have to live in the past, live at the moment since the past is history. Do not live in the future since that is a mystery. Be responsible for the present and make the future how you would want it to be. You are in control of your thoughts, and you need to make sure that you choose carefully what to accumulate in your brain and what should not. When you focus on living in the present, you will be aware of what you think and feel. That will help you to do away with the thoughts that are not helpful to you. You can interrupt them since you are aware of what is going on in your mind. Change your ideas to the present and how you want them to be, and they will, in turn, shape the future. Keep asking yourself whether you are living in the present and the exact thing that you want with your life.

Stay calm as well as confident

When you decide to responsible for your life, you will be more peaceful and you will have more confidence. Pay attention to making your life comfortable leaving alone all the things that make you lose your self-esteem. You will always be calm when you remember that no one is in control of your life, and you can choose how to respond to stimuli. You can want what to take from people and what to leave. You will have the confidence that you cannot fall into the trap of the past. When you control what you can, you will live a calm as well as healthy life.

See the good in people

Train yourself to see the right side of people so that you will not lose it, trying to put things in order. So, as you can have peace of mind, do not judge the rest on what you think they intend to do. Do not judge yourself, and by that, you will not have issues with your self-esteem. You need to understand where someone comes from so that you will not decide them. Do not label people according to how they look since that will make you treat them in a cruel way contrary to how it should be. When they realize that you are harsh on them, they will make life unbearable for you. When you pay attention to the positive side of a person, you will not find it hard to cope with living with them around you. When you have an easy time with the people around you, you will not forget what you aim to achieve in life. You need to see them as a fellow human being and give responses maturely. Do not just listen to provide a reply but instead look to understand. Ask questions where you need to understand something so that you do not just wait for the time that you will have the chance to interrupt. In that way, you will be fully responsible for your life to the extent that you can illuminate a conversation.

Stop blaming and complaining

You need to stop the blame game so that you can move forward and have a healthy life. Stop blaming everything that comes your way thinking that they are responsible for everything that is happening in your life. You are accountable, and you should not lose the focus if you want to be successful in life. When you accept full responsibility, you will move from being a victim to a victor. You can decide what to do when you are in a specific situation and know the exact role that you play. Complains are another way of blaming and behaving as if there is no choice. When you start complaining, you lack focus, and you think about how things are going wrong on you. Seek to learn from everything that is happening in your life rather than complaining when everything is not going right.

Take full responsibility

You are responsible for your thoughts, how you feel, your words as well as actions. It is how well you can be accountable for all this that you are going to create a good life. You have to accept that whatever you are thinking is from your mind. The way you feel is happening in your body, which is brought about by how you think. Do not wait for someone to force you to believe or do the thinking on your behalf. Similarly, to how you have no control over how a person will respond, it is the same way no one has control over the way you will react. You will react from your mindset, and you have to be responsible for any word that comes from your mouth.

For you to achieve your primary purpose, you need to work hard and be consistent. You may fail, but it will not be because you do not have the skills as well as the knowledge. It will be a real struggle if at all you want to make it in this hectic world. If you do not wish to be among the failures, you have to find a way on how to focus on your goals. Setting goals makes you feel energized but achieving the goals makes you feel confident with yourself. Find a way to maintain your passion as well as motivation so that you will make your dreams come true. Making use of these strategies will increase the probability of achieving the goals you have set.

However, you need to make sure that you are responsible for your life. Making yourself happy should be your main agenda. You need to realize that your happiness will not come from anywhere. It should precisely come from you since you are the only person who is responsible for your pleasure. Decide on being happy doing the things that will make you happy as well.

Overcoming Challenges

Life is full of challenges, and there is no way you can live without facing them here and there. It is not guaranteed that you will have funds at all times. There are times you will lack, and there are times you will even require means of getting these funds. However, this is the end of life. As a means of taking full responsibility for your life, you need to make a point of facing the challenges and devices factors of evading them. In other words, if you are having a financial crisis, you don't have to live in regrets as you beg for help from different individuals. However, you need to stand and look for ways you can fix the issue. The aspect indicates that you are adequately taking care of yourself and accountable for any aspect of life that occurs in your life. However, it is worth noting that different challenges have different means of evading them as well as facing them. You need to take the full charge pf your life and face challenges instead of avoiding the issue.

Take time to Reform

In most cases, when life pins one down, there are chances that one may feel dejected and lose focus in one way or another. It is worth noting that issues are there and calamities are real. In other words, one ought to realize that there are cases in life that are hurting, and some are destructive. However, you didn't have to live in problems and stay there. Instead, you need to take some time and heal. For instance, if you lose a relative or a friend, you need to take some time and Reform. Don't assume everything is okay and fail to create some time where you can relax and reflect on what to do next. The art of setting time apart after working is that it allows one to offload issues that might be affecting an individual. It is worth noting that the art of relaxation requires enough time to be effective.

Focusing on Important Content

Although life can be pissing, there is always a positive aspect that can be explored. In other words, in every calamity, there is a positive aspect that can be explored for life to be different. Thus, even if you fall in a ditch and there are no hopes of coming out of that hole alive, make a point of being optimists and take the challenge as an opportunity to learn and improve. Even if all your friends see negativity in all your approaches to life, you shouldn't give up. However, innovate the materials claimed uselessly and create something unique.

Embracing the Situation with a Positive Mind

Positivity is the key to the art of overcoming all sorts of challenges. In other words, you need to develop some sense of positivity that will enhance you see life from a different angle. In most cases, when one is insignificant lack, that when can determine whether they can take care of themselves. Low moments are quite some time important in learning who your real friends are. Thus, take any calamity as a learning opportunity and be prepared to improve on your character. It is worth noting that life can be sacking at times. However, the approach or rather the response of an individual determines whether they are capable of taking care of themselves. If one can absorb the shock of calamities and face life with an attitude of success and winning, reveal how effective one is taking responsibility if their life. In other words, the art of treating one's body well indicates that one is responsible. It is worth noting that even the art of accepting that something terrible has happened is a way of revealing that one is accountable for their lives.

Chapter 11: How to Make Stoicism the Foundation of Your Daily Routine

Stoicism is like a way of life, and therefore, for anyone who wants to be a stoic must incorporate stoic exercises in his or her life and make it as part of the daily routine. The daily activities should be guided by stoic exercises that lay a foundation of stoicism.

Meditate Daily

The best way to start the day is by waking up very early in the morning and put up a positive attitude that will keep you energized during the day. You should make sure that you have enough time and a quiet environment that will help you prepare for the day.

The room for preparing should not have much light, and as you sit down to make sure that you are comfortable enough. The day is ahead of you and it involves so many activities that need to be accomplished. It is good to go through all the activities of the day, and then register the challenges that come with the activities, and slowly by slowly reflecting on the challenges trying to find out the solutions to the challenges. Make sure that you know how each of the activities is going to be executed effectively. You should also have in mind something that you want to improve from the previous undertakings, as long as it is part of the activities to be executed. You also need inspiration, and therefore you can read writing that inspires you or a verse from the Bible, however, this depends on what inspires you as an individual. You can go through the inspirational writing several times, listening to it with your inner part of your heart.

Put it to yourself that after you go through the day, you should call yourself again back in a meditating room before you go to sleep and make sure that it is not brightly lit to give you a quiet moment without destructions. Go through the activities of the day, asking yourself what you did right and what you did wrong. Did you finish all the activities you intended to do for that day, and if there are activities that were left out, why were they left out. However, make sure that you accomplish all the activities that you had committed because you are living like today is the last day, if you carry today's activities in the next day, you might not get a chance to see tomorrow to do it. The activities that were not carried out should be rescheduled of there is still a chance of them being done. Congratulate yourself on what you did right and commit yourself to improve on what you did not do right when a chance presents itself. After the reflection on the day, you can clear your head and sleep.

Strive To Do What Is Good and Avoid What Is Bad

The daily activities involve making a decision about different issues, and therefore, as you go about your activities remember to be mindful in terms of the choices you make. Remember that every action regardless of whether it is considered important or not, has an ethical or moral component and for you to live a stoic life you must pursue virtue. Therefore, before you make any decision thought the day, make sure that it is directed towards making you virtuous. Put the many options that you have at hand to accomplish the activity and from the options, choose the one that is more moral.

You should also have deliberate activities that encourage doing good, it should be part of the plan, and not accidental. For instance, you can decide that after taking lunch, you make sure that you also provide lunch to one person that is in need. This does not mean that you should always provide lunch for someone; you can choose to do a different thing every day, but just make sure that you are doing it wholeheartedly.

Remember That All You Have Does Not Count

As you go about your daily activities, you must interact with other people from different levels of life, own different opinions, and have different strengths and weaknesses. The people also have different intellectual abilities and from different economic backgrounds. When you meet with them treat them with respect, because all that you have is not yours. Take all your possessions as borrowed things that you can lose any time. The good clothes that you wear, the food that you eat, the good health that you are enjoying, and all other possession including the people that you love should not be a basis for you to demean others; they can vanish in a fraction of a second. Therefore, regardless of your achievements, possession, and titles or the position you hold in whatever place, you are just a small thing on earth, which can vanish from the earth the effect felt by the whole world is small. Remember that even the prominent people die and it is only their names that are left in books to be read by people in the future generations. Therefore, as you mingle with people of different levels in different aspects remain focused; do not think of yourself highly because all of you are the same.

Take Time to Experience Hardship

There are conditions that you fear experiencing in your life, and because you know them, let yourself experience them bit by bit in your daily activities. For example, if you fear being demoted from the position you have to work as an ordinary worker, you can choose the activities done by the ordinary worker, and have a schedule that will help you do the tasks they do every day. The approach will help you appreciate the work done by the junior workers and deal with the anxiety and fear of losing the position that you have. The experience makes you realize that being at a lower position is not that bad, and because you have already lived it, it will be easy to cope in case it happens to you. The consistent discomfort that you feel when you practice being in hardship each day also brings about mental and physical endurance, and if a worst-case scenario comes your way, it will not leave you wretched.

Looking At Situation in the Wider Perspective

It is not always that we are happy or the events and situations that come our way in our daily activities are appealing; disappointment happens every day, and they can shut us from seeing the bright future that we have. When you are a disappointment, it does not matter the activity that has led to your disappointment with the person who has disappointed you. Sit down and look at yourself and what you are worth, and the life that you would wish to live in the future, and ask yourself, is looking miserable because of one person or one event in your life a good option. Count the blessing that surrounds you, and they cannot be compared to one disappointment. Therefore, always look at the future and not the past; the future can be made better, past time and all its activities cannot be rewound and made better. There is no need to dwell on the past, but the coming activities have greater potential. As a stoic always, take each opportunity in your routine seriously to improve your future.

Anticipating Negative Happenings

Before you begin your day, you have all the activities set. However, you should reflect on the plan for each activity and all the requirements for its effectiveness. As you evaluate, also look at the possibility of the activities failing or not going as you have planned. Also, anticipate the causes of the failure and look for measures to prevent it from falling. This might sound as being pessimistic, but it will save you from experiencing the actual failure because you have everything in place to prevent failure. In addition, since you are prepared for the failure, if it happens it does not affect you much. Therefore, in every plan that you have for the day, always anticipate negative happenings, and prepare for them by having measures to prevent them from happening.

Accepting What Happens

In a daily routine, sometimes things do not happen the way we have planned, this is because even though we plan for the daily activities, we do not have control of the way they would happen. Therefore, as you plan to keep in mind it might not be as planned, and if it happens as planned be happy about it, and if it does not happen as planned again be happy about it. There are things which are meant to happen the way they do, and even if you plan and take all the measures to make sure they happen as you wish, they still do not happen as expected. This means fate controls such situations, and it is good to accept them the way they happen. The attitude will help you not to spend much energy on things that cannot change, and not be frustrated when things do not happen as you wish. There is a reason that they happen the way they do, and even if you do not know the reason, it is always for the best.

Turning Problems into Blessings

It is not always that we encounter good experiences, there are bad experiences that come our way, and sometimes we ask ourselves why it should be me. When the experience is not good you should always learn to step on it and find a good experience from it. For instance, when going to work, you can meet people who step on you and just go away without apologizing. When you reach the workplace, the boss yells at you for no good reason. It seems unfair, but you can look at it as an opportunity to be more tolerant. Therefore, when you face a challenge in your daily routine, do not feel like, why me; take it as an opportunity to make yourself a better person.

Live Like Today Is Your Last Day

As you go about your daily routine, remember that you cannot live forever, and you do not know the day you will die. Therefore, think about your achievements when you die tomorrow. What will you have done for the world, including your friends, family members, and other people in general? How will you be remembered? This stoic practice will help you to maximize every minute of your time in a day by concentrating on what is more important, doing good things, and making the people you love and yourself happy. Remember that when you die you will not have such a chance; make use of the time you have on earth before it expires.

Do Not Engage In Judging Others

Different people have their choices and have a different view of life. When you see them engaging in certain activities that are not within your value system, understand that people are different and everybody has what he or she values in this life. When you hear a person talking, it is not good to quickly judge the person by only looking at what he or she says. Again, do not judge a group of people because of the misbehavior of one person. In addition, what is considered moral by a certain family or group might not be what you consider moral, and they are justified to hold their opinion on the same; who said your perspective of what is moral is universal. Let people do what they think is right and when they go astray, only learn from their mistakes and make yourself a better person. Therefore, you should always try to judge your way of doing things and make your life and relationship with other people better. Remember, the way other people behave is out of your control, but you should control the way you behave; therefore only judge your behavior and leave others to judge themselves. Judging others makes you sound as if you are superior moral something that is against stoicism principles.

Chapter 12: 52 Quotes to Inspire Your Year of Transformation

When a person decides to change or make an improvement in their personal life, quotes help a lot. The quotes help a person get through all the obstacles that may come along the way.

Pick a new quote every Monday to start your week right!

Week 1: You should never let go of something you cannot live without – Winston Churchill

This quote is meant to encourage someone to fight for something with all they have. People give up on things and people and then later on regret. Sometimes we let go when we are angry thinking that we made the right decision. But then when that thing or person is gone, we become very depressed. Therefore before letting go of something, we should consider the value it has in our lives.

Week 2: There's no life without failures and lessons- Unknown

This quote will help someone when they feel like giving up when things do not work as they had planned. Sometimes the downfalls are more than the achievement. However, these quotes encourage us to be positive-minded when we fall. To get all the lessons that come with the failures. If we never failed, we would never appreciate the small achievements we have in life.

Week 3: Success cannot be achieved by excuses- Unknown

It merely tells us that we either get the desired goals because we worked hard for them, or we get lazy and find excuses for not achieving them. If we work hard, we achieve; if we get lazy, we find excuses.

Week 4: People don't define who you are, you do! - Les Brown

People try to discourage you by making you feel like you are worthless. That, however, remains their opinion. What you think about yourself is what defines you because it is only you that knows your ability and your weaknesses.

Week 5: You are responsible for what you do- Les Brown

Most times, we find scapegoats for our failures in life when, in reality, it is us who are solely responsible for everything. It is easier to blame people or circumstances when we make poor decisions, but at the end of it, everyone is accountable for their actions.

Week 6: We live for the challenges in life – Joshua J.Marine

Sometimes we think that challenges make life our lives difficult. We are often asking for a life without problems. But imagine a life where everything went our way. There would be no hope and thrill for the next day. Therefore, we should appreciate every challenge and take it is a reason to fight on.

Week 6: You create your obstacles- Andrew Murphy

You are the only one that can set your limits. No one and nothing can stop you from achieving but yourself.

Week 7: Don't be someone you are not! Always be real to yourself!-Dr. Seuss

This means that you should be yourself. People who care for you will accept you the way you are. Most times, we find ourselves changing to fit in for the wrong people. People who will not appreciate any effort you make in having them around. So be you and let the real ones prove themselves.

Week 8: You are the difference, you need-John Kennedy

Change begins with us as individuals. What you feel needs change can only be changed if you take the first step. Most times, we leave it upon others to make the difference we want, yet you can also be the one to do it.

Week 9: If you don't get up, you become a failure."-Unknown

Everyone falls, but those who do not give up are not failures. It is only giving up that makes us losers.

Week 10: You only give up on what is not important for you- Unknown

Patience is hard, but one should look at what they will achieve for their patience. When you feel like giving up, you should focus on what you want, and that should keep you going.

Week 11: Patience is not enough; you have to act-Unknown

Waiting is good, but you should not just sit and wait. It is good to wait for something you know you are working hard for. There is much reward for waiting for something that you worked for instead of waiting to do nothing for things to fall into place.

Week 12: Create your own opportunities-Bruce Lee

Sometimes whatever you are looking for may be unachievable if you are expecting it from other people. There's nothing much you can do about that. But you can find your means to achieve it without relying on others.

Week 13: Nothing is permanent, don't expect happiness to be! - Denis Waitley

This encourages someone who feels unhappy that happiness is not permanent. Sometimes you are happy, but other times circumstances will make you feel miserable. Therefore, we should try to live every minute as it comes, thankfully so that we find something to be happy with.

Week 14: Don't worry when you fail, worry when you do not try-Jack Canfield

Failures provide lessons. Not trying does not give you experiences or achievements. Therefore a person who tries and fails is better than one who does not try.

Week 15: If you don't build yourself, you will build others- Unknown

If you do not see the potential in yourself, someone else will notice it. When others notice it, they will take advantage of you because they know how much you can help them achieve. Therefore it is important to explore our talents lest others abuse them.

Week 16: You are not happy because everything is right, you are happy because you decide to- Unknown

You cannot merely let circumstances determine your happiness. If you do, you will be so unhappy. You have to find a reason for you to be happy no matter the situation.

Week 17: You get to make your choices every morning-Unknown

This means that it is you who makes your own choices in chasing your goals. Your dreams may be right, but unless you work on them, they remain to be just dreams.

Week 18: You only overcome when you decide to act - Christopher Columbus

This means that if you want to move forward, you have to let go of the past. If you continue holding on to the past, it will keep pulling you backward, and therefore you will never achieve much.

Week 19: Help is given to those that seek it-Jesus

This means that you will only get help when you ask for it, look for it and go for it. No one will know you need help unless you do the above.

Week 20: You are who you want for yourself-Ralph Waldo Emerson

This quote means that you can be anything you want to be despite the circumstances surrounding you. Sometimes we think that we are destined to be what we are, but we can change destiny if we decide to.

Week 21: We accomplish what we never gave up on- Helen Kelle

This means that putting practice into something, we can achieve anything. It may seem impossible, but when we keep trying, we can attain anything.

Week 22: There is no defined perfect opportunity- Orison Swett Marden

This quote goes to explains that there are no great or small opportunities. What you do in any given circumstance is what matters. Some think that great things happen when given great opportunities, but any opportunity can produce great results if well utilized.

Week 23: Success has no straight path, but failure does, the path is making everyone happy-Herbert Bayard Swope

This means that trying to make everyone happy will make you fail. This is because when you are trying to please everyone, very many misleading ways will be used. It will, therefore, be challenging to have one leading way that will bring you success.

Week 24: Embrace every personal challenge and learn from it-L H.Murlin

Do not stress going through difficulties. Some challenges a learning ground, and one should seize every opportunity to gain experience to help them in the future.

Week 25: The dreamer dreams their dream and uses everything they have to accomplish it- Harriet Tubman

This encourages us to have great dreams. Sometimes we look at our goals and dismiss them, thinking that they are way too unachievable. However, there is no dream too big if you put everything you have to achieve it.

Week 26: Start small, use the little you have and give it your all-Arthur Ashe

This encourages us not to underestimate any opportunity. Grab the little things life gives; you never know what you could achieve.

Week 27: The limits to your dreams are fear - Les Brown

Our goals are only stopped by fear. If we put aside, nothing would hold us down.

Week 28: Dream while awake, dream when it's daytime, dream with your eyes open – T.E. Lawrence

This means that we all have dreams. The difference is what we do with our goals. While others stop at dreaming, others chase their dreams.

Week 29: There is no way to get back something already said, an opportunity when missed, and time when it's lost – Unknown

This means we should be careful with what we say because once we have spoken; there is no way of taking back what we said.

Week 30: You are the only sole happiness you need- David Burns

This means you can never derive happiness from anyone but yourself. If you decide to be happy, only you can make you happy.

Week 31: You can fix a problem by fixing your feelings about it-Unknown

One can decide what to do with a problem, if you let it break you down or if it helps you learn. Otherwise, a problem can be viewed as a lesson.

Week 32: Your actions distinguish you from your dreams- Unknown

This means your achievements will only be determined by your actions, so you have to act to achieve.

Week 33: Our regrets are our lack of willpower-Unknown

This quote tells us not to be scared of taking risks because if we don't take chances, we might regret it in the end.

Week 34: You are not your past; you are your future- Brian Tracy

Your background should not define you or make you stop dreaming. What matters is what you dream of in life.

Week 35: "The only person you should try to better than is the person you were yesterday."-Unknown

It means you should not compete with anyone; instead, you should try to improve yourself because that is all that matters.

Week 36: Don't let excuses waste your opportunities-Unknown

This means you can keep postponing doing something, but that will not gain you anything other waste than your time.

Week 37: You can achieve what you put to imaginations, and you can become whatever you want to be- William Arthur Ward

There is nothing in life that is unachievable if you set your mind and strength on it.

Week 38: The darkness lasts for a night, and the sun will always shine during the day- Unknown

It means nothing is permanent. No problem will stay with you forever. You will always get over the difficulties.

Week 39: We control our dreams from our minds, there anything is possible- Jamie Paolinetti

It means that all the barriers we experience are in mind. If we set our minds to achieve anything, there is nothing that would be difficult for us.

Week 40: Knock fear and watch it crash -Robin Sharma

This means that the only way to get rid of fear is by dealing with it instead of running away from it.

Week 41: Live life, love, get rid of anger, fight fear and treasure all the good memories - Unknown

This means we should appreciate everything life gives us by letting go of the negative things it throws us.

Week 42: Worry drinks your energy today - Corrie Ten Boom

This means that you will not achieve anything by worrying about the past, but you will only deny yourself the strength to face the present.

Week 43: Life is not measured in years, but years lived matter-Abraham Lincoln

It means that you should live life because you may live a long hopeless life while another may live a short yet remarkable life.

Week 44: Heroes are not people who never fell; heroes are people who rose after falling"- Confucius

It means that the greatest men are the ones that have failed many times yet moved past the fails. They never let failing stop define them.

Week 45: If you are preparing for something you are not aware of, you will fail-Seneca

This means that we should clear well-planned strategies because, without well-laid plans, we are likely to fail.

Week 46: Obstacles only stop people who are not serious, take away the sheep from the goats! - Randy Pausch

It means barriers only scare people who are not serious about their goals. Barriers separate those who really need it from those people who are playing about it.

Week 47: Stand-alone if you need to, don't forget to stand- Andy Biersack

It means you do not have to move with the majority if you believe in something. You can stand for what you believe in if you know you're right.

Week 48: Focus on the possibility and forget what if's - Unknown

Sometimes the negatives outweigh the positives, and this may make someone lose hope. But as long as you have something to hold on to, you should not give up.

Week 49: No plan means you get everything you never hoped for - Larry Winget

It means that if you do not have any goal, you will always have bad results. Therefore you have to have a plan to get positive results.

Week 50: Failure to try is the biggest failure- Unknown

You should always take risks, no matter what.

Week 51: You only need the right plan to get to live right - Unknown

It means that you should take advantage of every opportunity in life so that you avoid any regrets in life.

Week 52: You are more than a bad day - Unknown

This means that you should not let a single adverse situation determine your overall life because a bad status can change the next day.

Chapter 13: Essential Takeaways

From chapter one of this book, we learn how philosophy guides someone in various aspects of life. How it has successfully given people directions not by telling people exactly what to do. That would be awesome if we had a life guide that told us exactly what to do. But philosophy provides the direction which is equally essential because it gives the power of questioning things to determine what to do and what not to do. We learn to adopt the right attitude for life since that's all we have control over. Controlling our attitude means we get to interpret situations in life positively. Philosophy also teaches us that life has to have challenges, but that should never bring us down. We are able to ask ourselves the toughest question in the life of what's the worst that could happen. This prepares us beforehand to overcome anything mentally so that when reality hits us, we already know what to do.

Philosophy teaches us the power of positivity. That we are magnets and attract whatever we want by having the right attitude. It encourages us to wish ourselves the very best starting from our thoughts. Thinking positively, feeling positive, and expecting positive results while still considering the possibilities of worst scenarios. Then when the worst happens, not only are we mentally ready for it, we are able to let go. We are able to surrender to things that we know we really worked for but never achieved because they were beyond us. The power of letting go learned from philosophy saves our energy, and we become more energy to work on other things.

The second chapter teaches us about the values that will lead us not only to be the best for ourselves but also for others. We learn about stoicism and spirituality how they both help us know about the right and the bad things in life. Both help choose right over bad for ourselves as individuals and also for the people we live with. They teach us how to go about it diligently assessing things carefully so that we are mindful of others' feelings. Also, we learn to practice justice in all our endeavors, no matter how much influence we have and no matter how much power we have over others. We are taught to be fearless in everything we do because that is the only limit we have in us. Then both stoicism and spirituality teach us the discipline of self-control. Without control, we become hostile not only to ourselves but to others. We learn to stop ourselves when we have had enough of something before it becomes harmful. We learn to oblige to nature because all the values we need in life are deep within us.

Then we get to learn about stoicism and psychology, where we learn how to be moderate with our emotions. Stoicism encourages control of our feelings so that we are able to accept any given situations beyond us. Psychology helps people who are already too deep or about to get too deep in sufferings for lack of control for these emotions. Psychology encourages continuous practice to get rid of these emotions. Psychology helps the replacement of positivity in place of negativity in the hope that it eventually becomes a habit. That whenever we find ourselves feeling sad, we can always think of something that once made us happy, and we ultimately get happy. Therefore we learn how to control emotions by practicing the feelings we desire, and soon we will get them to become part of us.

In chapter four, we learn about the power of thinking more significant than ourselves. We learn to be mindful of other things other than ourselves because as much as we matter, others also matter. Being bigger than ourselves means going against and beyond our cages. We learn that there is more to life than who you are as an individual because we need others to help us out. We are able to appreciate that there is a source from which everything originates, and things do not just happen. Our purpose then becomes to agree with this so that we can appreciate that we are bigger and greater than what we actually see of ourselves. Knowing that though our lives are temporary and very short, there is so much, we can do for the world. There is so much that we can do to leave a legacy and also to achieve more than we ever thought possible.

We then learn how to practice objectivism where will let things flow on their own without trying to control them in any way. When we try to control things, we end up having undesired results. We learn that the best way to work out difficult things is by not worrying about them at all. We learn to disconnect our emotions from situations and letting them happen precisely as they are intended to happen. In so doing, we can assess the circumstances as they really because our feelings are not involved. When we are judging situations and involving our emotions, we tend to make impaired judgments and most likely to hurt other people in the process. But without our feelings involved, we are able to look at things from different points of view and therefore better results. This is a very important lesson for everyone in all life situations. It creates a platform for fairness. Thus there is no one trying to control things to get their desired results. This would work to helping solve cases whether socially or in courts of law. It is the best way to help solve the many human differences that exist. It is also a great lesson to use when trying to make crucial decisions in our lives — getting rid of our emotions first when in dilemmas and letting the right judgment win the day. Through objectiveness, we are also able to look at situations we are unable to make decisions on as if it was someone else going through them. When we see things from other people's eyes, we are able to help ourselves as if we were helping that person and therefore sober decisions. A neutral position provides a better judgment, and therefore there is unlikely to have discrepancies.

On learning to live according to human nature, we learn to adapt to our human needs. Human nature calls for the body to be fed when hungry. And for that, we should not deprive ourselves of food because that is going against nature. We should instead strive to go for things that make us better humans. We are responsible for conforming to our human needs as that is what makes grow and develop into better humans. This, therefore, means taking care of ourselves by eating right, exercising to keep fit and have a proper sleep. But this is not enough if we do not keep up with stoicism principles as this is also part of living according to human nature. But taking care of our biological demands and listening to our bodies when it asks for various things, including a holiday is the ultimate lesson. This is the only way we live according to who we as humans really are.

In chapter seven, we learn about letting go of the past and focusing on the present. Most times, we hold on to the pain that prevents us from moving on. This is because pain makes us afraid of trying; it discourages when you think that you could go through the same pain again. The problem of not letting go of the past is that it prevents us from seeing the potential of the present. Even if it is accomplishments, when we continue to focus on things we achieved in the past, we are unlikely to achieve right now. Some may argue that the past is only helpful in teaching us various lessons that we need. However, this is contradictory because time and circumstances change. What worked in the past might not work out now because there are other factors involved that changed. Focusing on the present helps you look at all the strategies and all the potentials involved that will help you get it right now. Letting go of the past means you forget everything else because for now, it doesn't count. The energy used in holding on to the past can be transformed into achieving much more today. The pain that we continue to carry from the past will only prevent you from opening up to new opportunities. There is so much to do today anyway, so when we hold on to the past, we only hinder ourselves from focusing on the present.

In chapter eight, we learn how to get unattached to external factors. We do not have much control over external factors and therefore, being emotionally attached will only hurt you. Learning to let go of what we cannot control gives us personal peace and happiness — especially when dealing with people because we cannot control their emotions. Detaching ourselves prevents us from frustrations when they do not think, act, or feel the way we do. Understanding that most pains come as a result of expecting too much from things we cannot control will help us get rid of those attachments.

Another essential lesson learned from this book is how to control the environment and live in perfect harmony. This means that we should take care of the environment so that it has something to give back to us. It is our obligation as human beings to do this, and we do not, the environment has a way of paying back. When we take care of the environment, we are protected from global warming, droughts, and we are able to save our animals, whether on land or in water.

Chapter ten teaches how to take charge of our lives. Some people use destiny as an excuse not to be responsible for their lives. Some even argue that a greater being is in charge, so there is, therefore, no need to try and be in control of one's life. However, everyone is in charge of their own life and all the decisions they make in life. If things didn't work out for you, it is you who is to blame for everything. And so does all the achievements that come your way. All your wins are a result of the charge you took in your life. If you sit around and wait for things to flow without action, you will fail, and you will be solely responsible for it. Being in charge means taking action where you are supposed to and letting the greater being take charge from the other end. Therefore this lesson is very important in making people know that they are responsible for their own actions.

The other essential takeaway is how to make stoicism a habit in our day to day lives. If we practiced stoicism, it would mean that we are able to feel for each other as human beings. We are fair to each other and also for ourselves; we are able to handle anything. Learning to make stoicism our habit toughens our physical self but toughens us mentally. We lose to gain, and there are happier in our lives. Make stoicism part of our daily lives enables us to have something to look forward to each day. We think of the day before it begins and can predict anything wrong that might happen and therefore be mentally prepared.

The final chapter gives us quotes that guide us through life. We all need some motivation to help us keep going. What motivation quotes do is strengthen us when we are almost giving up. They remind you of all the set goals and encourage you when things are falling apart. Without motivation, giving up seems so much easier because there is nothing to keep you going. It is essential to have a regular check on the quotes because they have a hidden meaning in them that will guide you through. When the day is hard, and you feel like you are almost giving up, going through your favorite quotes will help you. It's like adding yourself some fuel.